TERRITORY IN BIRD LIFE • HOWARD, H. ELIOT

	PAGE
CHAPTER I — Introduction	3
CHAPTER II — The Disposition to Secure a Territory	7
CHAPTER III — The Disposition to Defend the Territory	19
CHAPTER IV — The Relation of Song to the Territory	31
CHAPTER V — The Relation of the Territory to the System of Reproduction	42
CHAPTER VI — The Warfare between Different Species and its Relation to the Territory	53
CHAPTER VII — The Relation of the Territory to Migration	63
Index	73

ix

LIST OF ILLUSTRATIONS

Faces page

A pair of Lesser Spotted Woodpeckers attacking a Great Spotted Woodpecker *Frontispiece* 2

Territorial flight of the Black-tailed Godwit 54 15

Competition for territory is seldom more severe than individual Razorbills to secure positions on the among cliff-breeding seabirds, and the efforts of crowded ledges lead to desperate struggles 64 18

Male Blackbirds fighting for the possession of territory. The bare skin on the crown of the defeated bird shows the nature of the injuries from which it succumbed. 74 20

Male Cuckoos fighting before the arrival of a female 82 22

Two pairs of Pied Wagtails fighting in defence of their territories 86 23

Long-tailed Tit: males fighting for the possession of territory. The feathers have been torn from the crown of the defeated and dying rival 96 25

A battle between two pairs of Jays 106 28

The Female Chaffinch shares in the defence of the territory and attacks other females 110 29

Peregrine Falcon attacking a Raven 216 54

A battle between a pair of Green Woodpeckers and a Great Spotted Woodpecker for the possession of a hole in an oak-tree 238 59

Plans of the Water-meadow showing the Territories occupied by Lapwings in 1915 and 1916 *Between 58 and 59* 16

x-xi

SCIENTIFIC NAMES OF BIRDS MENTIONED IN THE TEXT

Raven *Corvus corax*.
Carrion-Crow *Corvus corone*.
Hooded Crow *Corvus cornix*.
Rook *Corvus frugilegus*.
Magpie *Pica pica*.
Jay *Garrulus glandarius rufitergum*.
Chough *Pyrrhocorax pyrrhocorax*.
Starling *Sturnus vulgaris*.
Greenfinch *Chloris chloris*.
Hawfinch *Coccothraustes coccothraustes*.
House-Sparrow *Passer domesticus*.
Chaffinch *Fringilla cœlebs*.
Brambling *Fringilla montifringilla*.
Linnet *Acanthis cannabina*.
Corn-Bunting *Emberiza calandra*.
Yellow Bunting *Emberiza citrinella*.
Cirl Bunting *Emberiza cirlus*.
Reed-Bunting *Emberiza schœniclus*.
Sky-Lark *Alauda arvensis*.
Pied Wagtail *Motacilla lugubris*.
Tree-Pipit *Anthus trivialis*.
Meadow-Pipit *Anthus pratensis*.
Great Titmouse *Parus major newtoni*.
Blue Titmouse *Parus cœruleus obscurus*.
Long-tailed Titmouse *Ægithalus caudatus roseus*.
Red-backed Shrike *Lanius collurio*.
Whitethroat *Sylvia communis*.

xii

Lesser Whitethroat *Sylvia curruca*.
Blackcap *Sylvia atricapilla*.
Grasshopper-Warbler *Locustella nœvia*.
Savi's Warbler *Locustella luscinioides*.
Reed-Warbler *Acrocephalus scirpaceus*.
Marsh-Warbler *Acrocephalus palustris*.
Sedge-Warbler *Acrocephalus schœnobœnus*.
Willow-Warbler *Phylloscopus trochilus*.
Wood-Warbler *Phylloscopus sibilatrix*.
Chiffchaff *Phylloscopus collybita*.
Song-Thrush *Turdus musicus clarkii*.
Redwing *Turdus iliacus*.
Blackbird *Turdus merula*.
Redstart *Phœnicurus phœnicurus*.
Redbreast *Erithacus rubecula melophilus*.
Nightingale *Luscinia megarhyncha*.
Stonechat *Saxicola rubicola*.

Whinchat *Saxicola rubetra.*
Wheatear *Œnanthe œnanthe.*
Hedge-Sparrow *Accentor modularis.*
Wren *Troglodytes troglodytes.*
Spotted Flycatcher *Muscicapa striata.*
Swallow *Hirundo rustica.*
Martin *Delichon urbica.*
Sand-Martin *Riparia riparia.*
Great Spotted Woodpecker *Dryobates major anglicus.*
Lesser Spotted Woodpecker *Dryobates minor.*
Green Woodpecker *Picus viridis.*
Cuckoo *Cuculus canorus.*
Tawny Owl *Strix aluco.*
Buzzard *Buteo buteo.*
Sparrow-Hawk *Accipiter nisus.*
Peregrine Falcon *Falco peregrinus.*
Merlin *Falco œsalon.*
Kestrel *Falco tinnunculus.*
xiii
Shag *Phalacrocorax graculus.*
Wild Duck *Anas boschas.*
Snipe *Gallinago gallinago.*
Dunlin *Tringa alpina.*
Ruff *Machetes pugnax.*
Redshank *Totanus totanus.*
Black-tailed Godwit *Limosa limosa.*
Curlew *Numenius arquata.*
Whimbrel *Numenius phæopus.*
American Golden Plover *Charadrius dominicus.*
Lapwing *Vanellus vanellus.*
Oyster-Catcher *Hæmatopus ostralegus.*
Herring-Gull *Larus argentatus.*
Kittiwake *Rissa tridactyla.*
Razorbill *Alca torda.*
Guillemot *Uria troille.*
Puffin *Fratercula arctica.*
Fulmar *Fulmarus glacialis.*
Water-Rail *Rallus aquaticus.*
Corn-Crake *Crex crex.*
Moor-Hen *Gallinula chloropus.*
Coot *Fulica atra.*
Wood-Pigeon *Columba palumbus.*
Turtle-Dove *Streptopelia turtur.*
Partridge *Perdix perdix.*
Black Grouse *Lyrurus tetrix britannicus.*
Red Grouse *Lagopus scoticus.*

Publisher's Note

Purchase of this book entitles you to a free trial membership in the publisher's book club at www.rarebooksclub.com. (Time limited offer.) Simply enter the barcode number from the back cover onto the membership form on our home page. The book club entitles you to select from millions of books at no additional charge. You can also download a digital copy of this and related books to read on the go. Simply enter the title or subject onto the search form to find them.

Note: This is an historic book. Pages numbers, where present in the text, refer to the first edition of the book and may also be in indexes.

If you have any questions, could you please be so kind as to consult our Frequently Asked Questions page at www.rarebooksclub.com/faqs.cfm? You are also welcome to contact us there.
Publisher: General Books LLC™, Memphis, TN, USA, 2012. ISBN: 9781153647854.
Proofreading: pgdp.net

※ ※ ※ ※ ※ ※ ※ ※

TRANSCRIBER'S NOTE:
There are a large number of compound words in this book including bird names which occur joined, spaced and hyphenated. No attempt has been made to correct these discrepancies as these are mostly alternative spellingd of thw same word. In the case of bird names it is difficult to decide as ornithologists are still debating on this subject.

TERRITORY IN BIRD LIFE

TERRITORY IN BIRD LIFE

BY H. ELIOT HOWARD

WITH ILLUSTRATIONS BY G. E. LODGE AND H. GRÖNVOLD

**NEW YORK
E. P. DUTTON AND COMPANY
1920**
v

A pair of Lesser Spotted Woodpeckers attacking a Great Spotted Woodpecker

Emery Walker ph.sc.

PREFACE

When studying the Warblers some twenty years ago, I became aware of the fact that each male isolates itself at the commencement of the breeding season and exercises dominion over a restricted area of ground. Further investigation, pursued with a view to ascertaining the relation of this particular mode of behaviour to the system of reproduction, led to my studying various species, not only those of close affinity, but those widely remote in the tree of avian life. The present work is the outcome of those investigations. In it I have endeavoured to interpret the prospective value of the behaviour, and to trace out the relationships in the organic and inorganic world which have determined its survival. Much is mere speculation; much with fuller knowledge may be found to be wrong. But I venture to hope that a nucleus will remain upon which a more complete territorial system may one day be established. vi

I have to thank Mr. G. E. Lodge and Mr. H. Grönvold for the trouble they have taken in executing my wishes; I also want to record my indebtedness to the late E. W. Hopewell; and to Professor Lloyd Morgan, F.R.S., I am beholden more than I can tell.
vii-viii

TERRITORY IN BIRD LIFE

CHAPTER I

INTRODUCTION

In his *Manual of Psychology* Dr Stout reminds us that "Human language is especially constructed to describe the mental states of human beings, and this means that it is especially constructed so as to mislead us when we attempt to describe the working of minds that differ in a great degree from the human."

The use of the word "territory" in connection with the sexual life of birds is open to the danger which we are here asked to guard against, and I propose, therefore, before attempting to establish the theory on general grounds, to give some explanation of what the word is intended to represent and some account of the exact position that representation is supposed to occupy in the drama of bird life.

The word is capable of much expansion. There cannot be territories without boundaries of some description; there cannot well be boundaries without disputes arising as to those boundaries; nor, one would imagine, can there be disputes without consciousness as a factor entering into the situation; and so on, until by 2 a simple mental process we conceive of a state in bird life analogous to that which we know to be customary amongst ourselves. Now, although the term "breeding territory," when applied to the sexual life of birds, is not altogether a happy one, it is difficult to know how otherwise to give expression to the facts observed. Let it then be clearly understood that the expression "securing a territory" is used to denote a process, or rather part of a process, which, in order to insure success to the individual in the attainment of reproduction, has been gradually evolved to meet the exigencies of diverse circumstances. Regarded thus, we avoid the risk of conceiving of the act of securing a territory as a detached event in the life of a bird, and avoid, I hope, the risk of a conception based upon the meaning of the word when used to describe human as opposed to animal procedure.

Success in the attainment of reproduction is rightly considered to be the goal towards which many processes in nature are tending. But what is meant by success? Is it determined by the actual discharge of the sexual function? So many and so wonderful are the contrivances which have slowly been evolved to insure this discharge, that it is scarcely surprising to find attention focused upon this one aspect of the problem. Yet a moment's reflection will show that so limited a definition of the term "success" can only be held to apply to certain forms of life; for where the young have to be cared for, 3 fostered, and protected from molestation for periods of varying lengths, the actual discharge of the sexual function marks but one stage in a process which can only succeed if all the contributory factors adequately meet the essential conditions of the continuance of the species.

Securing a territory is then part of a process which has for its goal the successful rearing of offspring. In this process the functioning of the primary impulse, the acquirement of a place suitable for breeding purposes, the advent of a female, the discharge of the sexual function, the construction of the nest, and the rearing of offspring follow one another in orderly sequence. But since we know so little of the organic changes which determine sexual behaviour, and have no means of ascertaining the nature of the impulse which is first aroused, we can only deal with the situation from the point at which the internal organic changes reflect themselves in the behaviour to a degree which is visible to an external observer. That point is reached when large numbers of species, forsaking the normal routine of existence to which they have been accustomed for some months, suddenly adopt a radical change in their mode of behaviour. How is this change made known to us? By vast numbers of individuals hurrying from one part of the globe to another, from one country to another, and even from mid-ocean to the coasts; by detachments travelling from one district to another; by isolated individuals deserting this place for 4 that; by all those movements, in fact, which the term migration, widely applied, is held to denote. Now the impulse which prompts these travelling hosts must be similar in kind whether the journey be long or short; and it were better, one would think, to regard such movements as a whole than to fix the attention on some one particular journey which fills us with amazement on account of the magnitude of the distance traversed or the nature of the difficulties overcome. For, after all, what does each individual seek? There may be some immature birds which, though they have not reached the necessary stage of development, happen to fall in with others in whom the impulse is strong and are led by them—they know not where. But the majority seek neither continent nor country, neither district nor locality is their aim, but a place wherein the rearing of offspring can be safely accomplished; and the search for this place is the earliest visible manifestation in many species of the reawakening of the sexual instinct.

The movements of each individual are then directed towards a similar goal, namely, the occupation of a definite station, and this involves for many species a distinct change in the routine of behaviour to which previously they had been accustomed. Observe, for example, one of the numerous flocks of Finches that roam about the fields throughout the winter. Though it may be composed of large numbers of individuals of different kinds, yet the various units form an amicable society actuated by 5 one motive—the procuring of food. And since it is to the advantage of all that the individual should be subordinated to the welfare of the community as a whole there is no dissension, apart from an occasional quarrel here and there.

In response, however, to some internal organic change, which occurs early in the season, individuality emerges as a factor in the developing situation, and one by one the males betake themselves to secluded positions, where each one, occupying a limited area, isolates itself from companions. Thereafter we no longer find that certain fields are tenanted by flocks of greater or less dimensions, while acres of land are uninhabited, but we observe that the hedgerows and thickets are divided up into so many territories, each one of which contains its owner. This procedure, with of course varying detail, is typical of that of many species that breed in Western Europe. And since such a radical departure from the normal routine of behaviour could scarcely appear generation after generation in so many widely divergent forms, and still be so uniform in occurrence each returning season, if it were not founded upon some congenital basis, it is probable that the journey, whether it be the extensive one of the Warbler or the short one of the Reed-Bunting, is undertaken in response to some inherited disposition, and probable also that the disposition bears some relation to the few acres in which the bird ultimately finds a resting place. Whilst for 6 the purpose of the theory I shall give expression to this behaviour in terms of that theory, and speak of it as a disposition to secure a territory, using the word disposition, which has been rendered current in recent discussion, for that part of the inherited nature which has been organised to subserve a specific biological purpose—strict compliance with the rules of psychological analysis requires a simpler definition; let us therefore say "disposition to remain in a particular place in a particular environment."

But even granting that this disposition forms part of the hereditary equipment of the bird, how is the process of reproduction furthered? The mere fact of remaining in or about a particular spot cannot render the attainment of reproduction any less arduous, and may indeed add to the difficulties, for any number of individuals might congregate together and mutually affect one another's interests. A second disposition comes, however, into functional activity at much the same stage of sexual development, and manifests itself in the male's intolerance of other individuals. And the two combined open up an avenue through which the individual can approach the goal of reproduction. In terms of the theory I shall refer to this second disposition as the one which is concerned with the defence of the territory.

Broadly speaking, these two dispositions may be regarded as the basis upon which the breed 7 ing territory is founded. Yet inasmuch as the survival value of the dispositions themselves must have depended upon the success of the process as a whole, it is manifest that peculiar significance must not be attached to just the area occupied, which happens to be so susceptible of observation; other contributory factors must also receive attention, for the process is but an order of relationships in which the various units have each had their share in determining the nature and course of subsequent process, so that, as Dr Stout says, when they were modified, it was modified.

Now the male inherits a disposition which leads it to remain in a restricted area, but the disposition cannot determine the extent of that area. How then are the boundaries fixed? That they are sometimes adhered to with remarkable precision, that they can only be encroached upon at the risk of a conflict—all of this can be observed with little difficulty. But if we regard them as so many lines definitely delimiting an area of which the bird is cognisant, we place the whole behaviour on a different level of mental development, and incidentally alter the complexion of the whole process. It would be a mistake, I think, to do this. Though conscious intention as a factor may enter the situation, there is no necessity for it to do so; there is no necessity, that is to say, for the bird to form a mental image of the area to be occupied and shape its course accordingly. The same result can be obtained without our having 8 recourse to so complex a principle of explanation, and that by the law of habit formation. In common with other animals, birds are subject to this law in a marked degree. An acquired mode of activity becomes by repetition ingrained in the life of the individual, so that an action performed to-day is liable to be repeated to-morrow so long as it does not prejudice the existence or annul the fertility of the individual.

Let us see how this may have operated in determining the limits of the area acquired, and for this purpose let us suppose that we are observing a male Reed-Bunting recently established in some secluded piece of marsh land. Scattered about this particular marsh are a number of small willows and young alder trees, each one of which is capable of providing plenty of branches suitable for the bird to perch upon, and all are in a like favourable position so far as the outlook therefrom is concerned. Well, we should expect to find that each respective tree would be made use of according to the position in which the bird happened to find itself. But what actually do we find—one tree singled out and resorted to with ever-increasing certainty until it becomes an important point in relation to the occupied area, a headquarters from which the bird advertises its presence by song, keeps watch upon the movements of its neighbours, and sets out for the purpose of securing food. We then take note of its wanderings in the immediate vicinity of the 9 headquarters, especially as regards the direction, frequency, and extent of the journeys; and we discover not only that these journeys proceed from and terminate in the special tree, but that there is a sameness about the actual path that is followed. The bird takes a short flight, searches a bush here and some rushes there, returns, and after a while repeats the performance; we on our part mark the extreme limits reached in each direction, and by continued observation discover that these limits are seldom exceeded, that definition grows more and more pronounced, and that by degrees the movements of the bird are confined within a restricted area. In outline, this is what happens in a host of cases. By repetition certain performances become stereotyped, certain paths fixed, and a routine is thus established which becomes increasingly definite as the season advances.

But while it would be quite untrue to

say that this routine is never departed from, and equally profitless to attempt to find a point beyond which the bird will under no circumstances wander, yet there is enough definition and more than enough to answer the purpose for which the territory has, I believe, been evolved, that is to say the biological end of reproduction. Again, however, the process of adjustment is a complex one. Habit plays its part in determining the boundaries in a rough and ready manner, but the congenital basis, which is to be found in the behaviour adapted 10 to a particular environment, is an important factor in the situation. For example, if instead of resting content with just a bare position sufficient for the purpose of reproduction, the Guillemot were to hustle its neighbours from adjoining ledges, the Guillemot as a species would probably disappear; or if instead of securing an area capable of supplying sufficient food both for itself and its young, the Chiffchaff were to confine itself to a single tree, and, after the manner of the Guillemot, trust to spasmodic excursions into neutral ground for the purpose of obtaining food, the Chiffchaff as a species would probably not endure. All such adjustments have, however, been brought about by relationships which have gradually become interwoven in the tissue of the race.

The intolerance that the male displays towards other individuals, usually of the same sex, leads to a vast amount of strife. Nowhere in the animal world are conflicts more frequent, more prolonged, and more determined than in the sexual life of birds; and though they are acknowledged to be an important factor in the life of the individual, yet there is much difference of opinion as to the exact position they occupy in the drama of bird life. Partly because they frequently happen to be in evidence, partly because they are numerically inferior, and partly, I suppose, because the competition thus created would be a means of maintaining efficiency, the females, by common consent, are supposed to supply the condition 11 under which the pugnacious nature of the male is rendered susceptible to appropriate stimulation. And so long as the evidence seemed to show that battles were confined to the male sex, so long were there grounds for hoping that their origin might be traced to such competition. But female fights with female, pair with pair, and, which is still more remarkable, a pair will attack a single male or a single female; moreover, males that reach their destination in advance of their prospective mates engage in serious warfare. How then is it possible to look upon the individuals of one sex as directly responsible for the strife amongst those of the other, or how can the female supply the necessary condition? As long as an attempt is made to explain it in terms of the female, the fighting will appear to be of a confused order; regard it, however, as part of a larger process which demands, amongst other essential conditions of the breeding situation, the occupation of a definite territory, and order will reign in place of confusion.

But even supposing that the male inherits a disposition to acquire a suitable area, even supposing that it inherits a disposition which results indirectly in the defence of that area, how does it obtain a mate? If the female behaved in a like manner, if she, too, were to isolate herself and remain in one place definitely, that would only add to the difficulties of mutual discovery. We find, however, in the migrants, that the males are earlier than the females 12 in reaching the breeding grounds, and, in resident species, that they desert the females and retire alone to their prospective territories, so that there is a difference in the behaviour of the sexes at the very commencement of the sexual process. What is the immediate consequence? Since the male isolates itself, it follows, if the union of the sexes is to be effected, that the discovery of a mate must rest largely with the female. This of course reverses the accepted course of procedure. But after all, what reason is there to suppose that, the male seeks the female, or that a mutual search takes place; what reason to think that this part of the process is subject to no control except such as may be supplied by the laws of chance?

Now, clearly, much will depend upon the rapidity with which the female can discover a male fit to breed; for if the course of reproduction is to flow smoothly, there must be neither undue delay nor waste of energy incurred in the search—some guidance is therefore necessary, some control in her external environment. Here the song, or the mechanically produced sound, comes into play, and assists in the attainment of this end. Nevertheless if every male were to make use of its powers whether it were in occupation of a territory or not, if the wandering individual had an equal chance of attracting a mate, then it would be idle to attempt to establish any relation between "song" on the one hand, and "territory" on 13 the other and impossible to regard the voice as the medium through which an effectual union of the sexes is procured. But there is reason to believe that the males utilise their powers of producing sound only under certain well-defined conditions. For instance, when they are on their way to the breeding grounds, or moving from locality to locality in search of isolation, or when they desert their territories temporarily, as certain of the residents often do, they are generally silent; but when they are in occupation of their territories they become vociferous— and this is notoriously the case during the early hours of the day, which is the period of maximum activity so far as sexual behaviour is concerned. So that just at the moment when the sexual impulse of the female is most susceptible to stimulation, the males are betraying their positions and are thus a guide to her movements. Nevertheless, even though she may have discovered a male ready to breed, success is not necessarily assured to her; for with multitudes of individuals striving to procreate their kind, it would be surprising if there were no clashing of interests, if no two females were ever to meet in the same occupied territory. Competition of this kind is not uncommon, and the final appeal is to the law of battle, just as an appeal to physical strength sometimes decides the question of the initial ownership of a territory.

I shall try to make clear the relations of the various parts to the whole with the 14 assistance of whatever facts I can command. I shall do so not only for the purposes of the theory, but because one so often finds the more important features of sexual behaviour regarded as so many distinct phenomena requiring separate treatment, whereas they are mutually dependent, and follow one another in ordered sequence. I spoke of the process as a series of relationships. Some of these relationships have already been touched upon; others will become apparent if we consider for a moment the purposes for which the territory has been evolved. Indirectly its purpose is that of the whole process, the rearing of offspring. But inasmuch as a certain measure of success could be attained, and that perhaps often, without all the complications introduced by the territory, there are manifestly advantages to be gained by its inclusion in the scheme. The difficulties which beset the path of reproduction are by no means always the same—all manner of adjustments have to be made to suit the needs of different species. There are direct relationships, such as we have been speaking of, which are essential to the every-day working of the process, and others which are indirect, though none the less important for they must have exercised an influence throughout the ages. These latter are furnished by the physical—the inorganic world, by climate, by the supply of the particular kind of breeding stations, by the scarcity or abundance of the necessary food and by the relative position of the food supply 15 to the places suitable for breeding. Why does the Reed-Bunting cling so tenaciously to an acre or more of marshy ground, while the Guillemot rests content with a few square feet on a particular ledge of rock? The answer is the same in both cases—to facilitate reproduction. But why should a small bird require so many square yards, whilst a very much larger one is satisfied with so small an area? The explanation must be sought in the conditions of existence. The Reed-Bunting has no difficulty in finding a position suitable for the construction of its nest; there are acres of waste land and reedy swamps capable of supplying food for large numbers of individuals, and the necessary situations for countless nests. But its young, like those of many another species, are born in a very helpless state. For all practical purposes they are without covering of any description and consequently require protection from the elements, warmth from the body of the brooding bird, and repeated supplies of nourishment. A threefold burden is thus imposed upon the parents: they must find food for themselves, they must afford protection to the young by brooding, and they must supply them with the necessary food at regular intervals. And their ability to do all this that is demanded of them will be severely taxed by the brooding which must perforce curtail the time available for the collection of food.

Let us then suppose that the Reed-Buntings 16 inhabiting a certain piece of marsh are divided into two classes, those which are pugnacious and intolerant of the approach of strangers, and those which welcome their presence. The nests of the former will be built in isolation, those of the latter in close proximity. In due course eggs will be laid and incubation performed, and thus far all alike will probably be successful. Here, however, a critical point is reached. If the young are to be freed from the risk of exposure, the parents must find the necessary supply of food rapidly. But manifestly all will not be in a like satisfactory position to accomplish this, for whereas the isolated pairs will have free access to all the food in the immediate vicinity of the nest, those which have built in proximity to one another, meeting competition in every direction, will be compelled to roam farther afield and waste much valuable time by doing so; and under conditions which can well be imagined, even this slight loss of time will be sufficient to impede the growth of the delicate offspring, or to lead perhaps to still greater disaster. If any one doubts this, let him first examine one of the fragile offspring; let him then study the conditions under which it is reared, observing the proportion of time it passes in sleep and the anxiety of the parent bird to brood; and finally let him picture to himself its plight in a wet season if, in order to collect the necessary food, the parents were obliged to absent themselves for periods of long duration.

17 Now take the case of the Guillemot. Its young at birth are by no means helpless in the sense that the young Reed-Bunting is, and food is readily procured. But breeding stations are scarce, for although there are many miles of cliff-bound coast, yet not every type of rock formation produces the fissures and ledges upon which the bird rests. Hence vast stretches of coast-line remain uninhabited, and the birds are forced to concentrate at certain points, where year after year they assemble in countless numbers from distant parts of the ocean. If, then, different individuals were to jostle one another from adjoining positions, and each one were to attempt to occupy a ledge in solitary State, not only would the successful ones gain no advantage from the additional space over which they exercised dominion, but inasmuch as many members that were fitted to breed would be precluded from doing so, the status of the species as a whole would be seriously affected. The amount of space occupied by each individual is therefore a matter of urgent importance. A few square feet of rock sufficient for the immediate purpose of incubation is all that can be allowed if the species is to maintain its position in the struggle for existence.

Our difficulty in estimating the importance of the various factors that make for success or failure arises from our inability to see more than a small part of the scene as it slowly unfolds itself. The peculiar circumstances under which these cliff-breeding forms dwell does, however, 18 enable us to picture, on the one hand, the precarious situation of an individual that was incapable of winning or holding a position at the accustomed breeding station, and, on the other, the plight of the species as a whole if each one exercised authority over too large an area. With the majority of species it is difficult to do this. So many square miles of suitable breeding ground are inhabited by so few Reed-Buntings that, even supposing certain members were to establish an ascendency over too wide an area, it would be impossible to discover by actual observation whether the race as a whole were being adversely affected. Competition doubtless varies at different periods and in different districts according to the numerical standing of the species in a given locality and according to the numerical standing of others that require similar conditions of existence; at times it may even be absent, just as at any moment it may become acute. These examples show how profoundly the evolution of the breeding territory may have been influenced by relationships in the inorganic world, and they give some idea of the intricate nature of the problem with which we have to deal.

I mentioned that the first visible manifestation of the revival of the sexual instinct was to be found in the movements undertaken by the males at the commencement of the breeding season. Such movements are characterised by a definiteness of purpose, whether they involve a protracted journey of 19 some hundreds of miles or merely embrace a parish or so in extent, and that purpose is the acquirement of a territory suitable for rearing offspring. They are thus directly related to the territory, and the question arises as to whether their origin may not be traced to such relatedness. So long as we fix our attention solely upon the magnitude of the distance traversed the suggestion may seem a fanciful one. Nevertheless, if the battles between males of the same species *are* directly related to the occupation of a position suitable for breeding purposes, if those which occur between males of closely related forms *can* be traced to a similar source, if the females take their share in the defence of the ground that is occupied, if, in short, the competition is as severe as I believe it to be, and is wholly responsible for the strife which is prevalent at the commencement of the breeding season—then such competition must have introduced profound modifications in the distribution of species; it must have even influenced the question of the survival of certain forms and the elimination of others; and since the powers of locomotion of a bird are so highly developed it must have led to an extension of breeding range, limited only by unfavourable conditions of existence.
20

CHAPTER II
THE DISPOSITION TO SECURE A TERRITORY

Those who have studied bird life throughout the year are aware that the distribution of individuals changes with the changing seasons. During autumn and winter, food is not so plentiful and can only be found in certain places, and so, partly by force of circumstances and partly on account of the gregarious instinct which then comes into functional activity, different individuals are drawn together and form flocks of greater or less dimensions, which come and go according to the prevailing climatic conditions. But with the advent of spring a change comes over the scene: flocks disperse, family parties break up, summer migrants begin to arrive, and the hedgerows and plantations are suddenly quickened into life. The silence of the winter is broken by an outburst of song from the throats of many different species, and individuals appear in their old haunts and vie with one another in advertising their presence by the aid of whatever vocal powers they happen to possess—the Woodpecker utters its monotonous call from the accustomed oak; the 21 Missel-Thrush, perched upon the topmost branches of the elm, persistently repeats its few wild notes; and the Swallow returns to the barn.

All of this we observe each season, and our thoughts probably travel to the delicate piece of architecture in the undergrowth, or to the hole excavated with such skill in the tree trunk; to the beautifully shaped eggs; to the parent birds carrying out their work with devoted zeal—in fact, to the whole series of events which complete the sexual life of the individual; and the attachment of a particular bird to a particular spot is readily accounted for in terms of one or other of the emotions which centre round the human home.

But if this behaviour is to be understood aright; if, that is to say, the exact position it occupies in the drama of bird life is to be properly determined, and its biological significance estimated at its true value, it is above all things necessary to refrain from appealing to any one of the emotions which we are accustomed to associate with ourselves unless our ground for doing so is more than ordinarily secure. I shall try to show that, in the case of many species, the male inherits a disposition to secure a territory; or, inasmuch as the word "secure" carries with it too much prospective meaning, a disposition to remain in a particular place when the appropriate time arrives.

If the part which the breeding territory plays in the sexual life of birds is the important one I believe it to be, it follows that the 22 necessary physiological condition must arise at an early stage in the cycle of events which follow one another in ordered sequence and make towards the goal of reproduction, and that the behaviour to which it leads must be one of the earliest visible manifestations of the seasonal development of the sexual instinct. When does this seasonal development occur? For how long does the instinct lie dormant? In some species there is evidence of this first step in the process of reproduction early in February; there is reason to believe that in others the latter part of January is the period of revival; and the possibility must not be overlooked of still earlier awakenings, marked with little definiteness, though nevertheless of sufficient strength to call into functional activity the primary impulse in the sexual cycle. Here, then, we meet with a difficulty so far as direct observation is concerned, for the duration of the period of dormancy and the precise date of revival vary in different species; and, if accurate information is to be obtained, the study of the series of events which culminate in the attainment of reproduction ought certainly to begin the moment behaviour is influenced by the internal changes, whatever they may be, which are responsible for the awakening of the sexual instinct.

In considering how this difficulty might be met, the importance of migratory species as a channel of information was gradually borne in upon me; for it seemed that the definiteness [23] with which the initial stage in the sexual process was marked off, as a result of the incidence of migration, would go far towards removing much of the obscurity which appeared to surround the earlier stages of the breeding problem in the case of resident species. Recent observation has shown that I exaggerated this difficulty, and that it is generally possible to determine with reasonable accuracy the approximate date at which the internal changes begin to exert an influence on the behaviour of resident species also. Nevertheless, the specialised behaviour of the migrants furnished a clue, and pointed out the direction which further inquiry ought to take.

Those who are accustomed to notice the arrival of the migrants are aware that the woods, thickets, and marshes do not suddenly become occupied by large numbers of individuals, but that the process of "filling up" is a gradual one. An individual appears here, another there; then after a pause there is a further addition, and so on with increasing volume until the tide reaches its maximum, then activity wanes, and the slowly decreasing number of fresh arrivals passes unnoticed in the wealth of new life that everywhere forces itself upon our attention. If now, instead of surveying the migrants as a whole, our attention be directed to one species only, this gradual arrival of single individuals in their accustomed haunts will become even more apparent; and if the investigation be pursued still further and these single individuals observed [24] more closely, it will be found that in nearly every case they belong to the male sex. Males therefore arrive before females. This does not mean, however, that the respective times of arrival of the males and females belonging to any one species are definitely divided, for males continue to arrive even after some of the females have reached their destination; and thus a certain amount of overlapping occurs. A truer definition of the order of migration would be as follows:— Some males arrive before others, and some females arrive before others, but on the average males arrive before females. This fact has long been known. Gätke refers to it in his *Birds of Heligoland*. "Here in Heligoland," he says, "the forerunners of the spring migration are invariably old males; a week or two later, solitary old females make their appearance; and after several weeks, both sexes occur mixed, *i.e.*, females and younger males; while finally only young birds of the previous year are met with." Newton alludes to it as follows:—"It has been ascertained by repeated observation that in the spring movement of most species of the northern hemisphere, the cock birds are always in the van of the advancing army, and that they appear some days, or perhaps weeks, before the hens"; and Dr Eagle Clarke, in his *Studies in Bird Migration*, makes the following statement:—"Another characteristic of the spring is that the males, the more ardent suitors, of most species, travel in advance of the females, and arrive at their meeting quarters some days, it is said in some [25] cases even weeks, before their consorts." Some interesting details were given in *British Birds* [1] in regard to the sex of the migrants that were killed by striking the lantern at the Tuskar Rock, Co. Wexford, on the 30th April 1914. In all, there were twenty-four Whitethroats, nine Willow-Warblers, eight Sedge-Warblers, and six Wheatears; and on dissection it was found that twenty Whitethroats, seven Willow-Warblers, eight Sedge-Warblers, and one Wheatear were males.

What a curious departure this seems from the usual custom in the animal world! Here we have the spectacle afforded us of the males, in whom presumably the sexual instinct has awakened, deserting the females just at the moment when we might reasonably expect their impulse to accompany them would be strongest; and this because of their inherited disposition to reach the breeding grounds. If, in order to attain to reproduction, the male depended primarily upon securing a female— whether by winning or fighting matters not at the moment—if her possession constituted the sole difference in his external environment between success and failure, then surely one would suppose that an advantage must rest with those individuals which, instead of rushing forward and inflicting upon themselves a life of temporary isolation, remained with the females and increased their opportunities for developing that mutual appreciation which, by some, is held to be a [26] necessary prelude to the completion of the sexual act, and to which close companionship would tend to impart a stimulus.

In thus speaking, however, we assume that the revival of the sexual instinct in the migratory male is coincident in time with its return to the breeding quarters; and we do so because the act of migrating is believed to be the first step in the breeding process. But it is well to bear in mind just how much of this assumption is based upon fact, and how much is due to questionable inference. All that can be definitely asserted is this, that appropriate dissection reveals in most of the migrants, upon arrival at their destination, unquestionable evidence of seasonal increase in the size of the sexual organs. Beyond this there is nothing to go upon. Yet if the term "sexual instinct" is held to comprise the whole series of complex relationships which are manifest to us in numerous and specialised modes of behaviour, which ultimately lead to reproduction, and which have gradually become interwoven in the tissue of the race, there can be little doubt that the assumption is a reasonable one. To some, the term may recall the fierce conflicts which are characteristic of the season; to others, emotional response; to not a few, perhaps, the actual discharge of the sexual function—all of these, it is true, are different aspects of the one instinct;

but at the same time each one marks a stage in the process, and the different stages follow one another in ordered sequence. However, we are not concerned at the moment with the term in 27 its wider application; we wish to know the precise stage at which the disposition to mate influences the behaviour of the male. Is the female to him, from the moment the seasonal change in his sexual organs takes place, a goal that at all costs must be attained? Or is it only when the cycle of events which leads up to reproduction is nearing completion that she looms upon his horizon? One would like to be in a position to answer these questions, but there is nothing in the way of experimental evidence to go upon; and if I say that there is reason to believe that, in the earlier stages, the female is but a shadow in the external environment of the male, it must be taken merely as an expression of opinion, though based in some measure upon a general observation of the behaviour of various species.

Before attempting to explain the difference in the times of arrival of the male and female migrant, let us examine the behaviour of some resident species at a corresponding period. My investigations have been made principally amongst the smaller species—the Finches and the Buntings—which often pass the winter in or near the localities wherein they brought up offspring or were reared. It is true that they wander from one field to another according to the abundance or scarcity of food; it is also true that, if the weather is of a type which precludes the possibility of finding the necessary food, these wanderings may become extensive or even develop into partial migrations. But under the 28 normal climatic conditions which prevail in many parts of Britain, these smaller resident species seem to find all that they require without travelling any great distance from their breeding haunts. Flocks composed of Yellow Buntings, Cirl Buntings, Corn-Buntings, Chaffinches, Greenfinches, etc., can be observed round the farmsteads or upon arable land; small flocks of Reed-Buntings take up their abode on pieces of waste land and remain there until the supply of food is exhausted, deserting their feeding ground only towards evening when they retire to the nearest reed-bed to pass the night; flocks of Hawfinches visit the same holly-trees day after day so long as there is an abundance of berries on the ground beneath; and so on.

I have mentioned the Reed-Bunting; let us take it as our first example and try to follow its movements when the influence exerted by the internal secretions begins to be reflected on the course of its behaviour. First, it will be necessary to discover the exact localities in any given district to which the species habitually returns for the purpose of procreation; otherwise the earlier symptoms of any disposition to secure a territory may quite possibly be overlooked in the search for its breeding haunts.

In open weather Reed-Buntings pass the winter either singly, in twos or threes, or in small flocks, on bare arable ground, upon seed fields, or in the vicinity of water-courses; but in the breeding season they resort to marshy 29 ground where the *Juncus communis* grows in abundance, to the dense masses of the common reed (*Arundo phragmites*), and such like places. During the winter, the male's routine of existence is of a somewhat monotonous order, limited to the necessary search for food during the few short hours of daylight and enforced inactivity during the longer hours of darkness. But towards the middle of February a distinct change manifests itself in the bird's behaviour. Observe what then happens. When they leave the reed-bed in the morning, instead of flying with their companions to the accustomed feeding grounds, the males isolate themselves and scatter in different directions. The purpose of their behaviour is not, however, to find fresh feeding grounds, nor even to search for food as they have been wont to do, but rather to discover stations suitable for the purpose of breeding; and, having done so, each male behaves in a like manner—it selects some willow, alder, or prominent reed, and, perching thereon, leads a quiet life, singing or preening its feathers. Now if the movements of one particular male are kept in view, it will be noticed that only part of its time is spent in its territory. At intervals it disappears. I do not mean that one merely loses sight of it, but that it actually deserts its territory. As if seized with a sudden impulse it rises into the air and flies away, often for a considerable distance and often in the same direction, and is absent for a period which may vary in length from a few minutes to an hour 30 or even more. But these periodical desertions become progressively less and less frequent in occurrence until the whole of its life is spent in the few acres in which it has established itself.

The behaviour of the Yellow Bunting is similar. In any roadside hedge two or more males can generally be found within a short distance of one another, and in such a place their movements can be closely and conveniently followed. Under normal conditions the ordinary winter routine continues until early in February; but the male then deserts the flock, seeks a position of its own, and becomes isolated from its companions. Now the position which it selects does not, as a rule, embrace a very large area—a few acres perhaps at the most. But there is always some one point which is singled out and resorted to with marked frequency—a tree, a bush, a gate-post, a railing, anything in fact which can form a convenient perch, and eventually it becomes a central part of the bird's environment. Here it spends the greater part of its time, here it utters its song persistently, and here it keeps watch upon intruders. The process of establishment is nevertheless a gradual one. The male does not appear in its few acres suddenly and remain there permanently as does the migrant; at first it may not even roost in the prospective territory. The course of procedure is somewhat as follows:—At dawn it arrives and for a while utters its song, preens its feathers, or searches for food; then it vanishes, 31 rising into the air and flying in one fixed direction as far as the eye can follow, until it becomes a speck upon the horizon and is ultimately lost to view. During these excursions it rejoins the small composite flocks which still frequent the fields and farm buildings. For a time the hedgerow is deserted and the bird remains with its companions. But one does not have to wait long for the return; it reappears as suddenly as it vanished, flying straight back to the few acres which constitute its territory, back even to the same gate-post or railing, where it again sings. This simple routine may be repeated quite a number of times during the first two hours or so of daylight, with, of course, a certain amount of variation; on one occasion the bird may be away for a few minutes only, on another for perhaps half an hour, whilst sometimes it will fly for a few hundred yards, hesitate, and then return—all of which shows clearly enough that these few acres possess some peculiar significance and are capable of exercising a powerful influence upon the course of its behaviour. And so the disposition in relation to the territory becomes dominant in the life of the bird.

Or take the case of the Chaffinch. In winter large or small flocks can be found in many varied situations. But in the latter part of February, or the early days of March, these flocks begin to disperse. At daylight males can then be observed in all kinds of situations, either calling loudly, uttering their spring note, 32 or exercising their vocal powers to the full; and it will be found that, in the majority of instances, these males are solitary individuals, that they pass the early hours of the morning alone, and that their normal routine of calling, singing, or searching for food, is only interrupted by quarrels with their neighbours. The same locality is visited regularly—not only the same acre or so of ground, but even the same elm or oak, has, as its daily occupant, the same cock Chaffinch. And temporary desertions from the territory occur also, much like those referred to in the life of the Bunting, but perhaps not so frequently. One has grown so accustomed during the dark days of winter to the sociable side of Chaffinch behaviour—to the large flocks searching for food, to the endless stream of individuals returning in the evening to roost in the holly-trees, to the absence of song—that this radical departure from the normal routine comes as something of a surprise; for the days are still short, the temperature is still low, the nesting season is still many weeks ahead, and yet for part of the day, and for just that part when the promptings of hunger must be strongest, the male, instead of joining the flock, isolates itself and expends a good deal of energy in insuring that its isolation shall be complete. And in place of the silence we hear from all directions the cheerful song uttered with such marked persistency that it almost seems as if the bird itself must be aware that by doing so it was advertising the 33 fact of its occupation of a territory. This is surely a remarkable change, and the females in the meantime continue their winter routine.

One other example. The monotonous call of the Greenfinch is probably familiar to all. In winter these birds accompany other Finches and form with them flocks of varying sizes, but in the spring the flocks disperse, and the Greenfinch, in common with other units of the flock, alters its mode of life. But whereas the Chaffinch or the Bunting begins to acquire its territory in February, the Greenfinch only does so in April. When the organic changes do at length begin to make themselves felt, the male seeks a position of its own, and having found one remains there, uttering its characteristic call. But owing probably to the fact that it is much later than the aforementioned species in acquiring a territory, temporary desertions are not so much in evidence. The species is so very plentiful, and the bird is so prone to nest in gardens and shrubberies surrounding human habitations, that this seasonal change in its routine of existence cannot fail to be noticed. One can hear its call in every direction, one can watch the same individual in the same tree; and it is the male that is thus seen and heard, the female appears later. Thus the behaviour falls into line with that of the Bunting or the Chaffinch.

The behaviour of these resident species throws some light upon the early arrival of the 34 males which we are endeavouring to explain in the case of the migrants. Let us see how their actions compare. The male resident deserts the female early in the year and establishes itself in a definite position, where it advertises its presence by song; the male migrant travels from a great distance, arrives later, and also establishes itself in a definite position, where it, too, advertises its presence by song. The male resident passes only the earlier part of the day in its territory at the commencement of the period of occupation; the male migrant remains there continuously from the moment it arrives. The male resident deserts its territory at intervals, even in the morning; the male migrant betrays no inclination to do so. Thus there is a very close correspondence between the behaviour of the two, and what difference there is—slight after all—cannot be said to affect the main biological end of securing territory. One is apt to think of the problem of migration in terms of the species instead of in terms of the individual. One pictures a vast army of birds travelling each spring over many miles of sea and land, and finally establishing themselves in different quarters of the globe; and so it comes about, I suppose, that a country or some well-defined but extensive area is regarded as the destination, the ultimate goal, of the wanderers. But the resident male has a journey to perform, short though it may be; it, too, has a destination to reach, neither a country nor a locality, but a place wherein the rearing of offspring can 35 be safely accomplished, and it, too, arrives in that place in advance of the female.

With these facts at our disposal, we will endeavour to find an explanation. It is unlikely that specialised behaviour would occur in generation after generation under such widely divergent conditions, and, moreover, expose the birds to risk of special dangers, if it were but an hereditary peculiarity to which no meaning could be attached. Hence the appearance of the males in their breeding haunts ahead of the females becomes a fact of some importance, and suggests that the extensive journey in the one case, and the short journey in the other, may both have a similar biological end to serve.

Darwin evidently attached importance to this difference between the males and the females in their times of arrival. In the *Descent of Man* he referred to it as follows: "Those males which annually first migrated in any country, or which in spring were first ready to breed, or were the most eager, would leave the largest number of offspring; and these would tend to inherit similar instincts and constitutions. It must be borne in mind that it would have been impossible to change very materially the time of sexual maturity in the females without at the same time interfering with the period of the production of the young—a period which must be determined by the season of the year." Newton suggested the following explanation [2]: "It is not difficult to [36] imagine that, in the course of a journey prolonged through some 50° or 60° of latitude, the stronger individuals should outstrip the weaker by a very perceptible distance, and it can hardly be doubted that in most species the males are stouter, as they are bigger than the females." Granting that the males are the stronger, how can this account for their outstripping the females by a week, ten days, or even a fortnight, in a journey of perhaps 1500 miles? To expect the birds to accomplish such a distance in seven days is surely not estimating their capabilities too highly, and any slight inequality in the power of flight or endurance could give the males an advantage of a few hours only. But this explanation, based upon inequalities in the power of flight and endurance on the one hand, and the magnitude of the distance traversed on the other, cannot afford a solution of the behaviour of the resident males, and is less likely, therefore, to be a true solution of that of the migrants.

There is another theory, simple enough in its way, which will probably occur to many. It is based on the assumption that the males reach sexual maturity before the females; and it is contended that the functioning of the instincts which contribute towards the biological end of reproduction depend upon the organic changes which the term "sexual maturity" is held to embrace, and that, inasmuch as the migratory instinct belongs to the group of such instincts, [37] the males must be the first to leave their winter quarters.

What is meant by the "migratory instinct"? To speak of it as one of the instincts concerned in reproduction is not enough. Reproduction involves the actual discharge of the sexual function, which involves the females; but the first visible manifestation of organic change in the male is its desertion of the females. Yet this is the behaviour which is referred to as the "migratory instinct," and which comes into play, according to this theory, because the bird has reached sexual maturity. Manifestly we must have some clear understanding as to what these terms represent. That organic changes determine the functioning of certain definite instincts at certain specified times there can be no doubt; that these changes may occur at a somewhat earlier date in the male than in the female is more than probable, but that this explains the behaviour in question I do not believe. One wants to know why the changes should occur earlier in the male, what disposition it is which first comes into functional activity, and to what such disposition is related.

It may, however, be urged that, after all, this apparent eagerness to reach the breeding grounds is but a modification of hereditary procedure under the guiding hand of experience. What more likely result would follow from the enjoyment associated with previous success in the attainment of reproduction than a craving to repeat the experience? What stronger incentive [38] to a hurried return could be imagined? It must be admitted that there are certain facts which might be used in support of an appeal to experience as a reasonable explanation. For example, the first males to arrive often display that richness of colouring which is generally supposed to indicate a fuller maturity. Gätke even speaks of the "most handsome old birds being invariably the first to hasten back to their old homes." But if experience is a factor, if some dim recollection of the past is held to explain the hurried departure of the male migrant, one wants to know with what such recollection is associated. Is it associated with the former female, or with the former breeding place, or with both? I take it that any recollection, no matter how vague, must be primarily associated with the particular place wherein reproduction had previously been accomplished; and I grant that if the first individuals to appear were invariably the older and experienced birds, their early return might be explained on the basis of such an association. But if there is reason to believe that a proportion are young birds on the verge of carrying out their instinctive routine for the first time, then we cannot appeal to past experience in explanation of their behaviour.

The age of a bird is difficult to determine. Experience leads me to believe that some of the males that arrive before the females are birds born the previous season; one finds, for instance, individuals with plumage of a duller hue, [39] which denotes immaturity, amongst the first batch of arrivals. But though plumage may sometimes be a satisfactory guide, yet to rely upon it alone, or upon a more perfect development of feather, is to exceed the limits of safety. How, then, can we ascertain whether all the males that arrive before the females have had some previous experience of reproduction? Well, we take a particular locality and note the migrants that visit it year after year, and we find that the respective numbers of the different species are subject to wide annual fluctuations. Not every species lends itself to an inquiry of this kind: some are always plentiful and fluctuation is consequently difficult to discern; others are scarce and variation is easily determined. Those which are of local distribution but conspicuous by their plumage, or easily traced by the beauty or the peculiarity of their song, afford the more suitable subjects for investigation. For example, the Grasshopper-Warbler, Marsh-Warbler, Nightingale, Comcrake, Red-backed Shrike, or Whinchat have each some distinctive peculiarity which makes them conspicuous, and each one is subject to marked fluctuation in numbers. The small plantation or wooded bank may hold a Nightingale one year, but we miss its song there the next; the osier bed or gorse-covered common which vibrates with the trill of the Grasshopper-Warbler one April is deserted the following season; the plantation which is occupied by a host of common migrants this summer may be enlivened 40 next year by the song of the rarer Marsh-Warbler also; and so on. The fluctuation is considerable: we observe desertion on the one hand, appropriation on the other, and yet males appear before females whether the particular plantation, osier bed, or swamp had been inhabited or not the previous season. This fact is not without significance. It shows that similar conditions prevail both amongst the males that appropriate breeding grounds new to them, and amongst those that return to some well-established haunt; and on the assumption that the earlier arrivals are experienced males, the same birds evidently do not return to the same place year after year. Granting, then, that the males which appropriate new breeding-grounds are young birds, how can their earlier arrival be explained in terms of past experience; and granting that they are old, and therefore experienced, how can it be explained in terms of association?

Again, it may be urged that if there is some biological end to be furthered by this hurried return, and if recollection of past experience is a means towards that end, such recollection need not necessarily be associated with a definite place, but only in a vague way with the whole series of events leading up to reproduction—in which series the migratory journey may even have acquired meaning. Whether there be any recollection of a previous journey or of a nest with young, I do not know. But the young bird is capable of performing its journey, of 41 building its nest, and of rearing its young antecedent to experience—racial preparation has fitted it thus far; why then exclude the other event in the series, the earlier departure of the male, from hereditary equipment? If the journey were a casual affair without any goal attaching to it, if the males upon arrival wandered about in search of a mate, there would be some ground for thinking that a vague recollection of the whole former experience was sufficient to explain the hurried return; but since the pleasurable effect of association, founded upon previous experience of a definite place, cannot well be established, and since it is so difficult to study the objective aspect of the behaviour in question without coming to the conclusion that the journey is related to the appropriation of a place suitable for the rearing of offspring, one is tempted to ask whether the hurried return may not also be so related.

Now the males of some of the migratory species, especially of those which are accustomed to return to their breeding haunts early in the season, are called upon to face greater dangers and have a greater strain imposed upon their strength by starting forth upon their journey ten days or a fortnight before their prospective mates. The blizzards which so often sweep across the northern parts of Europe in the latter half of March, destroying in their course the all too scanty supply of insect life, may take toll of their numbers; or the westerly gales, which are not infrequent at that period, 42 may meet them in mid-ocean and add to the perils of their journey; or the temperature of the previous weeks may have been sufficiently low to arrest the development of insect life—and yet males are annually exposed to these risks in hurrying to their breeding grounds. For what purpose? The answer will largely depend upon the way in which we regard those few acres wherein a resting place is ultimately found. For myself, I believe that they are of importance, inasmuch as the securing of a place suitable for the rearing of offspring is a primary condition of success in the attainment of reproduction; and if this be so, it is evident that the interests of the race will be better served by the males making good this first step before the females are ready to pair, otherwise they might oscillate between two modes of behaviour, created by the premature functioning of conflicting impulses.

The different steps in the process seem to follow one another in ordered sequence. The male inherits a disposition—which for us, of course, has prospective meaning—to seek the appropriate breeding ground and there to establish itself; and as early a functioning of this disposition as possible, consonant with the conditions of existence in the external environment, may have been evolved for the following reasons—firstly, the earlier individuals will meet with less interference wherever they may settle, every locality will be open to them, every acre free, their only need being that 43 particular environment for which racial preparation has fitted them. In the second place, being already established when other males appear upon the scene, and advertising their presence by song, they will be less liable to molestation; thirdly, in those cases in which a long journey is undertaken, they will have ample time to recover from the fatigue, and, if attacked by later arrivals, will thus be in a better position to defend their territories; and lastly, a greater uniformity in their distribution will be insured before the females begin their search.

There is, besides, another good reason for thinking that the earlier males will have an advantage. We will assume—and from the abundant evidence supplied by the marking of birds, it is quite a reasonable assumption—that there is a tendency, generally speaking, for individuals to return to the neighbourhood of their birthplace, or to the place in which they had previously reared their offspring. Now the earlier arrivals will have no difficulty in securing territories; those that come later may have to search more diligently, still they will gain all that they require so long as any available space remains. Then comes the point when all suitable ground is occupied, and yet there are males to be provided for. What will be the position of these males? Urged by their inherited nature, they will leave the district and possibly continue their search into those adjoining, only, however, to add to the diffi 44 culties of the males there similarly situated; and even allowing that they are at length successful in establishing themselves, what are their prospects of securing mates? Since the earlier females will not extend their wanderings farther than is absolutely necessary, but will pair whenever the opportunity for doing so arises, it is to the later females, forced onwards by competition, that the late males must look for mates; so that when at length pairing does take place, much valuable time will have been lost.

The disadvantages which the late arrivals have to face are therefore great, and it is probable that the percentage which attain to reproduction will on the average be somewhat lower than the percentage in the case of the earlier arrivals. The district in which my observations have been made lies well within the limits of the breeding range of most of our common species, and it is not surprising that I should have met with little evidence of failure to breed as a result of failure to secure territory. Some interesting information was supplied to me, however, by the late Robert Service. He found, in certain seasons in Dumfriesshire, flocks of from ten to fifty unmated Sedge-Warblers, which, from the time of their arrival in May until the middle of July, haunted reed-filled spaces along stagnant streams. These flocks appeared to him to be composed of loosely-attached individuals of a migrant flock that had failed to find things 45 congenial enough to entice them to disperse. But may they not have been composed of males that had failed to secure territories, or of females that had failed to discover males in possession of territories, or of both?

We have seen that, in the case of many species, each male establishes itself in a particular place at the commencement of the breeding season, even though this may mean a partial or perhaps a complete severance from former companions. We must now discuss this fact in greater detail because it is opposed to the views often held regarding the sexual behaviour of birds, and is manifestly of importance when considering the theory of breeding territory.

First, however, there is a point which requires some explanation. I speak of the *same* male being in the *same* place. How can I prove its identity? In the first place it is highly improbable that a bird which roams about within the same small area of ground, makes regular use of a certain tree and a certain branch of that tree, and observes a similar routine day after day, can be other than the same individual. But, apart from this general consideration, are there any means by which individuals of the same species can be identified? Well, there is variation in the plumage. Supposing we take a dozen cock Chaffinches and examine them carefully, we shall find slight differences in pattern and in colour—more grey 46 here or a duller red there, as the case may be—and though these differences may not be sufficient to enable us to pick out a bird at a distance, they are nevertheless conspicuous when it is close at hand. Then again there is variation in the song; and the more highly developed the vocal powers the greater scope there is for variation. But even the phrases of a simple song can be split up and recombined in different ways. If one were asked casually whether the different phrases of the Reed-Bunting's song always followed one another in the same sequence, the answer would probably be that they certainly did so, whereas the bird is capable of combining the few notes it possesses in a surprising number of different ways. And lastly, there are differences in just the particular way in which specific behaviour, founded upon a congenital basis, is adapted by each individual to its own special environment. Racial preparation determines behaviour as a whole, but the individual is allowed some latitude in the execution of details which are in themselves of small moment—the selection of a particular tree as a headquarters and a particular branch upon that tree, the direction of the distant excursion, and the direction of the limited wanderings within the small area surrounding the headquarters which in the course of time determine the extent of the territory, are matters for each individual to decide when the occasion for doing so arises. Moreover instances of abnormal coloration or abnormal song are not 47 rare, and they are valuable since they place the identity of the individual beyond dispute. I can recall the case of a Willow-Warbler whose song was unlike that of its own or any other species, and of a Redbreast whose voice puzzled me not a little. I can recollect also a male Yellow Bunting whose foot was injured or deformed. Of this bird's behaviour I kept a record for two months or so; and inasmuch as it inhabited a roadside hedge, and was of fearless disposition, the deformed foot could plainly be seen whenever it settled upon the road to search for food. Identification is not, therefore, a difficulty. There is always some small difference in colour or in song, or some well-defined routine which makes recognition possible.

Owing to their great powers of locomotion, birds have generally been regarded as wanderers more or less; anything in the nature of a fixed abode, apart from the actual nest, having been accounted foreign to their mode of life; and even the locality immediately surrounding the nest has not been apprehended as possessing any meaning for the owner of that nest. No doubt the supply of food determines their movements for a considerable part of the year; they seek it where they can find it, here to-day, there to-morrow—in fact few species fail to move their quarters at one season or another, so that there is much truth in the notion that birds are wanderers. Yet to suppose that every individual one sees or hears—every Lapwing on the meadow, or Nightingale in the withy 48 bed—is in that particular spot just because it happens to alight there as it roams from place to place, is to take a view which the observed facts do not support. For as soon as the question of reproduction dominates the situation, a new condition arises, and the habits formed during the previous months are reversed, and the males, avoiding one another, or even becoming actively hostile, prefer a life of seclusion to their former gregariousness—all of which occurs just at the moment when we might reasonably expect them to exhibit an increased liveliness and restlessness as a result of their endeavour to secure mates; and so universal is the change that it might almost be described as an accompaniment of the sexual life of birds generally.

That the Raven and certain birds of prey exert an influence over the particular area which they inhabit has long been known, and it has been recognised more especially in the case of the Peregrine Falcon, possibly because the bird lives in a wild and attractive country, and, forcing itself under the notice of naturalists, has thus had a larger share of attention devoted to its habits. Moreover, when a species is represented by comparatively few individuals, and each pair occupies a comparatively large tract of country, it is a simple matter to trace the movements and analyse the behaviour of the birds. There is a rocky headland in the north-west of Co. Donegal comprising some seven miles or so of cliffs, where three pairs of Falcons and two pairs of Ravens have nested for many years. 49 Each year the different pairs have been more or less successful in rearing their young; each year the young can be seen accompanying their parents up to the time when the sexual instinct arises; and yet the actual number of pairs is on the whole remarkably constant, and there is no perceptible increase. It seems as if the numbers of three and two respectively were the maximum the headland could maintain. But this is no exceptional case; it represents fairly the conditions which obtain as a rule amongst those species, granting, of course, a certain amount of variation in the size of each territory determined by the exigencies of diverse circumstances.

If we take a given district, and devote our attention to the smaller migrants that visit Western Europe each returning spring for the purpose of procreation, we shall find that the movements of the males are subject to a very definite routine. This, however, is not true of every male; some may be wending their way to breeding grounds at a distance; others may be seeking the particular environment to which they may be adapted; others again, having found their old haunts destroyed, may consequently be seeking new.

Of all this there is evidence. Small parties of Chiffchaffs pass through a district on their way to other breeding grounds, flitting from hedge to hedge as they move in a definite direction with apparently a definite purpose; Reed-Warblers settle in a garden or plantation, 50 eminently unsuited to their requirements, and disappear; Wood-Warblers arrive in some old haunt, and finding it no longer suitable for their purpose, seek new ground. So that plenty of individuals are always to be found, which, for the time being at least, are wanderers.

In the district which I have in mind, the wandering males form only a small part of the incoming bird population. The majority of individuals that fall under observation are those that have made this particular district their destination; and in doing so, they may possibly have been guided by their experience as owners or inmates of former nests, for it cannot be doubted that a return to the neighbourhood of the birthplace would lead to a more uniform distribution and therefore be advantageous, and the tendency to do so might consequently have become interwoven in the tissue of the race. How, then, do they behave? A certain amount of movement, an interchanging of positions, even though restricted to an area defined, let us say, by experience, might be expected under the circumstances—that, however, is not what we find; we observe the available situations plotted out into so many territories, each one of which is occupied by a male who passes the whole of his time therein. Take whatever species we will—Whitethroat, Whinchat, Willow-Warbler, Red-backed Shrike, it matters not which, for there is no essential difference in the general course of procedure—this condition will be found to prevail. Generally speaking, the 51 behaviour in relation to the territory can be studied more conveniently where a number of individuals of the same species have established themselves in proximity to one another. Such species as the Chiffchaff, Willow-Warbler, or Wood-Warbler are often sufficiently common to allow of three or more of their respective males being kept in view at the same time; and the disposition to occupy a definite position can be readily observed. The Reed-Warbler is a suitable subject for an investigation of this kind; for since it is restricted by its habits to localities wherein the common reed (*Arundo phragmites*) grows in abundance, and since such localities are none too plentiful and often limited in extent, the area occupied by each individual is necessarily small—if it were not so the species would become extinct. Hence it is a simple matter to study the routine of the different individuals and to mark the extent of their wanderings.

In this way the males of all the Warblers that breed commonly in Great Britain establish themselves, each one in its respective station at the respective breeding ground; so, too, do those of many other migrants—for example, the Whinchat, Wheatear, Tree-Pipit, and Red-backed Shrike. All of these, it is true, are common species—numbers of individuals can often be found in close proximity—and therefore it may be argued that they keep to one position more from pressure of population than from any inherited disposition working towards that end. 52 But the rarer species behave similarly. Districts frequented by the Marsh-Warbler and offering plenty of situations of the type required by the bird are often inhabited by a few members only, and yet the disposition to remain in a definite position is just as marked.

You will say, however, that these smaller migrants have no exceptional powers of flight; that they have besides just completed a long and arduous journey; and you will ask why they should be expected to wander, whether it is not more reasonable to expect that, in order to overcome their fatigue, they should remain where they settle. The Cuckoo is a wanderer in the wider sense of the term, and is gifted with considerable powers of flight. Upon arrival the male flies briskly from field to field, showing but little signs of weariness; yet we have only to follow its movements for a few days in succession to assure ourselves that the bird is no longer a wanderer; for just as the Warbler or the Chat moves only within a definitely delimited area, so the male Cuckoo, strange as it may seem, restricts itself to a particular tract of land. The area over which it wanders is often considerable and consequently it is not possible to keep the bird always in view, but inasmuch as the variation in the voices of different individuals is quite appreciable, identification is really a simple matter. If we cannot keep the bird in sight, we can trace its movements by sound and mark the extent of its wanderings, which by repetition become more and more 53 defined, until a belt of trees here, or an orchard there, mark a rough and rarely passed boundary line.

Let us take another example from the larger migrants—the Black-tailed Godwit, a bird common enough in the Dutch marshes but no longer breeding in this country. On suitable stretches of marsh land, numbers will be found in proximity one to another after the manner of the Lapwing, each male occupying a definite space of ground wherein it passes the time preening, searching for food, or in sleep—though at the same time keeping a strict watch over its territory. Now the preference shown for a particular piece of ground, and the determination with which it is resorted to, is the more remarkable when we take into consideration the specific emotional behaviour arising from the seasonal sexual condition. This behaviour is expressed in a peculiar flight. The bird rises high in the air, circles round with slowly beating wings above the marsh, and utters a call which, as far as my experience goes, is characteristic of the performance. The air is often full of individuals circling thus even beyond the confines of the marsh, for a male does not limit its flight to a space immediately above its territory; but nevertheless careful observation will show how unerringly each one returns to its own position on the breeding ground, no matter how extensive the aerial excursion may have been. And so, when the males of the smaller migrants confine their 54 movements to an acre of ground at the completion of their long journey, they are acting no more under the influence of fatigue than the Cuckoo, which keeps within certain bounds yet flies about briskly, or the Godwit which, though holding to its few square yards on the ground, executes most tiring and extensive flights above the marsh.

Of all the migrants, however, the behaviour of the Ruff is perhaps the most strange, and though it has long been known that these birds have their special meeting places where they perform antics and engage in serious strife, yet it is only within recent years that the primary purpose of these gatherings has been ascertained—that purpose being the actual discharge of the sexual function. Mr. Edmund Selous has carried out some exhaustive investigations into their activities at the meeting places, and he makes it clear that each bird has its allotted position. He says, for example, that "It begins to look as though different birds had little seraglios of their own in different parts of the ground," that "each Ruff has certainly a place of its own," or again that "this Ruff indeed, which I think must be a tender-foot, does not seem to have a place of its own like the others." Nevertheless it is only at the meeting places that they have their special positions; there is no evidence to show that each one has a special territory, wherein it seeks its food, as the Warbler has, and therefore some may think that we are here confronted with behaviour of a 55 different order. But we must bear in mind that the process has been adjusted to meet the requirements of different species: the size of the territory, the period of its daily occupation, the purpose which it serves—these all depend upon manifold relationships and do not affect the principle. Why it has been differentiated in different circumstances we shall have occasion to discuss later; for the moment it is enough that at the end of its migratory journey each Ruff occupies one position on the meeting ground.

Territorial flight of the Black-tailed Godwit

Now birds that are paired for life, whose food-supply is not affected by alternations of climate, have no occasion to desert the locality wherein they have reared their offspring, and so their movements, being subject to a routine which would tend to become increasingly definite, must in the course of time and according to the law of habit formation become organised into the behaviour we observe. Is it necessary, therefore, to seek an explanation of their tendency to remain in one place in anything so complex as an inherited disposition? Again, since we have to confess to so very much ignorance on so many points connected with the whole phenomenon of migration, may there not be some condition, hitherto shrouded in mystery, which might place so different a complexion on the corresponding aspect of migrant behaviour as to rid us, in their case also, of the necessity of appealing to an inherited disposition? Such questions are justifiable. And if the life-histories 56 of other species gave no further support to our interpretation, if, in short, the evidence were to break down at this point, then we should be forced to seek some other explanation more in keeping with the general body of facts.

But far from placing any obstacle in the way of an interpretation in terms of inherited disposition, the behaviour of many of those residents which are not paired for life gives us even surer ground for that belief. Moreover in their case the initial stages in the process are more accessible to observation. I will endeavour to explain why. In the process of reproduction the environment has its part to play—whether in the manner here suggested, or indirectly through the question of food-supply, matters not at the moment. Now, migratory species are more highly specialised than resident species as regards food, and are affected more by variations of temperature, so that they can live for only a part of the year in the countries which they visit for the purpose of procreation. Hence the organic changes, which set the whole process in motion, must be coincident in time with the growth of appropriate conditions in the environment; for if it were not so, if the internal organic changes were to develop prematurely, the bird would undertake its journey only to find an insufficiency of food upon its arrival, and this would scarcely contribute towards survival. Definite limitations have therefore been imposed upon the period of organic change. But in the 57 case of many resident species the conditions are somewhat different, for they remain in the same locality throughout the year, and a gradual unfolding of the reproductive process cannot therefore have a similarly harmful effect. Thus it comes about that the behaviour of the migrant, when it arrives at the breeding ground and first falls under observation, represents a stage in the process which, in the case of the resident, is only reached by slow degrees; and by closely observing the behaviour as it is presented to us in the life of the resident male, we not only gain a better insight into the changes in operation, but can actually witness the breaking down of the winter routine, stereotyped through repetition, by the new disposition as it arises.

The first visible manifestations, even though they may be characterised by a certain amount of vagueness, are therefore of great importance if the behaviour is to be interpreted aright; and in order to insure that none of these earlier symptoms shall be missed, it is necessary to begin the daily record of the bird's movements at an early date in the season. As a rule the second week in February is sufficiently early for the purpose, but the date varies according to the prevailing climatic conditions. Even in species widely remote there is great similarity of procedure, and the behaviour of the Buntings is typical of that of many. With the rise of the appropriate organic state the male resorts at daybreak to a suitable environment, occupies a 58 definite position, and singling out some tree or prominent bush, which will serve as a headquarters, advertises its presence there by song. At first the bird restricts its visits, which though frequent in occurrence are of short duration, for the most part to the early hours of the morning; it disappears as suddenly as it appeared, and one can trace its flight to the feeding grounds—a homestead or perhaps some newly sown field. But by degrees the impulse to seek the society of the flock grows less and less pronounced, the visits to the territory are more and more prolonged, and the occupation of it then becomes the outstanding feature of the bird's existence. This in outline is the course of procedure as it appears to an external observer.

But although much can be learnt from the lives of these smaller species, there is no gain-saying the fact that a great deal of patient observation is required, and the process is apt to become tedious. There are others, however, which are more readily observed, whilst their life-histories afford just as clear an insight into the effect produced by the new disposition upon the developing situation; and among these the Lapwing takes a prominent position, because it is plentiful and inhabits open ground where it is easily kept in view.

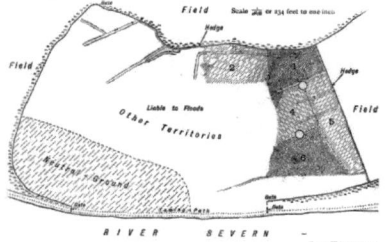

Plans of the Water-meadow showing the Territories occupied by Lapwings in 1915.

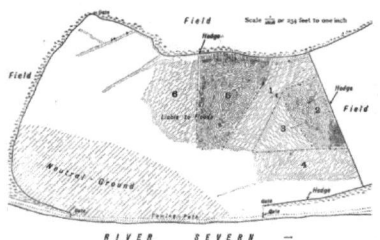

Plans of the Water-meadow showing the Territories occupied by Lapwings in 1916

There is a water meadow with which I am familiar, where large numbers resort annually for the purpose of procreation. Here they begin to arrive towards the end of February, 59 and at first collect in a small flock at one end of the meadow. A male, here and there, can then be seen to break away from the flock, and to establish itself in a definite position upon the unoccupied portion of the ground, where it remains isolated from its companions. Others do likewise until the greater part of the meadow is divided into territories. Six of these territories I kept under observation for approximately two months in the year 1915. The occupant of the one marked No. 6 upon the 1915 plan was a lame bird, a fortunate occurrence as it enabled me to follow its movements with some accuracy; and though it maintained its position for some weeks, it ultimately disappeared, as a result, I believe, of the persistent attacks of neighbouring males. The behaviour of the males during the first fortnight or so after they broke away from the flock was interesting. Though they retired to their territories and remained in them for the greater part of their time, yet it was only by degrees that they finally severed their connection with the flock, for so long as a nucleus of a flock remained, so long were they liable to desert their territories temporarily and to rejoin their companions.

Lapwings, as is well known, collect in flocks during the winter months, and these flocks, which sometimes reach vast proportions, are to be found on tidal estuaries, water meadows, arable land, and such like places, according to the prevailing climatic conditions. This flocking 60 may contribute towards survival, and may therefore be the result of congenital dispositions which have been determined on biological grounds. On the other hand, since food at that season is only to be obtained in a limited number of situations, the birds may be simply drawn together by accident. In the former case the behaviour would be instinctive, in the latter, though accidental at first, recurrent repetition would tend to make it habitual; but in either case the impulse to accompany the flock must be a powerful one, for on the one hand it would depend upon inherited, and on the other hand upon acquired, connections in the nervous system. Now observe that soon after the flock arrived in the meadow, single males detached themselves; there was no hesitation, they just retired from their companions and settled in their respective territories. They were not expelled, for if their leaving had been compulsory much commotion would have preceded their departure, and their return would certainly not have been welcomed. A reference to the plan will make the position clearer; the neutral zone inhabited by the flock is there shown as situated in one corner of the meadow, the territories that fell under observation are plotted out as far as possible to scale, and the more important zones of conflict are also marked.

The males spent part of their time in their respective territories and part with the flock, so long as it remained in existence. When a 61 male was in its territory it avoided companions and was openly hostile to intruders; when it was with the flock it wandered about with companions in search of food. The contrast between the two modes of behaviour was very marked, and it was evident that the gregarious instinct was gradually yielding its position of importance to the new factor—the territory. If there had been no flock, if a few solitary individuals had appeared here and there and had established themselves in different parts of the meadow, one would have had no definite evidence of the strength of the impulse in the male to seek a position of its own, one could only have argued from the general fact of males flocking in the winter and isolating themselves in spring that something more than accident was required to explain so radical a change. But since the birds returned in a flock to the ground upon which they intended to breed, and since the flock occupied temporarily part of the ground whilst the partitioning of the remainder was still proceeding, it was possible to gauge the strength of the impulse, which was forcing the males to isolate themselves in particular areas of ground, by comparing it with the impulse to accompany the flock—and the measure of its intensity was the rapidity with which the latter impulse yielded its position of importance.

Like the Lapwing, the Coot and Moor-Hen are easily kept under observation, and since many individuals often breed in proximity, 62 more than one can be watched at the same moment; moreover the area occupied by each male generally embraces an open piece of water as well as part of the fringe of reeds, so that the movements of the bird can be followed without much difficulty. Under favourable conditions manifestations of the developing situation become visible at a comparatively early date in the season—the middle or the latter part of February—and these manifestations resemble those of other species. But the Moor-Hen passes summer and winter alike in the same situation, and being therefore in a position to respond at once to internal stimulation, however vague, the change from the one state to the other is gradual. This, however, is a matter of detail; the main consideration lies in the fact that the impulse to retire to a definite position, to avoid companions, and to live in seclusion, is strongly marked, and produces a type of behaviour similar on the whole to that of the Lapwing. First of all there is the appropriation of a certain position, the limits of which are fixed according to the law of habit formation, and according to the pressure exerted by neighbouring individuals; then there is the neutral ground over which the birds wander amicably in search of food; and finally there is the contrast between the pugnacity of the male whilst in its territory, and its comparative friendliness when upon neutral ground.

Evidence of similar behaviour is to be found 63 in the life of the Black Grouse, a bird which has always excited the curiosity of naturalists on account of the special meeting places to which both sexes resort in the spring. Mr. Edmund Selous watched these birds in Scandinavia, where he kept a daily record at one of the meeting places. In various passages he refers to the appropriation of particular positions by particular males, and concludes thus: "It would seem from this that, like the Ruffs, each male Blackcock has its particular domain on the assembly ground, though the size of this is in proportion to the much greater space of the whole. On the other mornings, too, the same birds, as I now make no doubt they are, have flown down into approximately the same areas."

The cliff-breeding species—Guillemots, Razorbills, and Puffins—are difficult to investigate because individuals vary so little, and the sexes resemble one another so closely; yet, despite these difficulties, we can gain some idea of the general purport of their activities. But when the ledges are crowded and the air is filled with countless multitudes, how is it possible to keep a single bird in view for a sufficient length of time to understand its routine? The difficulty is not an insuperable one. The flights, undertaken seemingly for no particular purpose, are often of short duration and are completed before the strain of observation becomes too great; moreover an individual sometimes possesses a special mark or characteristic which serves to 64 make it conspicuous. For example, there is a well-marked variety of the Common Guillemot, the Ringed or Bridled Guillemot of science, distinguished by an unusual development of white round the eye and along the furrow behind it. One such individual I was fortunate in discovering upon a crowded cliff, and, as in the case of the Lapwing with the broken leg or the Yellow Bunting with the injured foot, the identity of the bird was beyond dispute, and one could observe that it appropriated to itself a particular position upon a particular ledge.

Guillemots and Razorbills return at intervals to the breeding stations early in the season, and these visits are repeated with growing frequency until the birds are finally established. I have witnessed these periodic returns during March in the south of England, and during April in the north-west of Ireland, and I am informed that in the latter district such visits may occur as early as February. Gätke, who had ample opportunity of observing the birds in Heligoland, puts their return at an even earlier date. "They visit their breeding places," he says, "in flocks of thousands at the New Year, often even as early as December, as though they wanted to make sure of their former haunts being well preserved and ready for their reception." Such visits, however, are irregular in occurrence; the birds arrive, and, after spending a short time upon the ledges, disappear. And since there is not the same evidence in their coming and going 65 of that method which we observe in the periodical returns of the Bunting or the Finch, it may be thought that needless importance is being attached to an episode in their lives which is quite intelligible in terms of a feeble response determined by a dawning organic change. While it may be quite intelligible in such terms it is not thereby explained; for every response must have as its antecedent an inherited connection in the nervous system determined on biological grounds. Besides, these early periodic returns conform in general to the type of behaviour displayed by other species, the males of which return to their breeding grounds many weeks before the real business of reproduction begins. Are we then justified in regarding them as accidents of the developing situation? Are we not rather bound to admit that they have some definite biological end to serve?

These examples show that the males of many species reverse their mode of life at the commencement of the breeding season and proceed to isolate them-

Composition for territory is seldom more severe than amongst cliff-breeding sea birds, and the efforts of individual Razorbills to secure positions on the crowded ledges lead to desperate struggles.

Emery Walker ph. sc

selves, each one in a definitely delimited area.

There are three ways in which we may attempt to interpret this particular mode of male behaviour. We may regard it as an accidental circumstance, nowise influencing the course of subsequent procedure; or, appealing to the law of habit formation, we may regard it as an individual acquirement; or 66 again, we may invest it with a deeper significance and seek its origin in some specific congenital disposition determined on purely biological grounds.

Which of these three shall we choose? The first by itself requires but little consideration; for though it might explain the initial visit, it cannot account for the persistency with which the plot of ground is afterwards resorted to. Supposing, however, that we combine the first and the second; supposing, that is to say, we assume, for the purpose of argument, that the initial visit is fortuitous, and that constancy is supplied by habit formation—would that be a satisfactory interpretation? It is a simple one, inasmuch as it only requires that a male shall alight by chance in a particular place for a few mornings in succession in order that the process may be set in motion. Now an essential condition of habit formation is recurrent repetition; given this repetition and, it is true, any mode of activity is liable to become firmly established. But how can we explain the repetition? Even if we are justified in assuming that the initial visit is purely an accidental occurrence, we cannot presume too far upon the laws of chance and assume that the repetition, at first, is also fortuitous.

So that we come back to the congenital basis, the last of our three propositions. And it will, I think, be admitted that the facts give us some grounds for believing that the securing of the territory has its root in the inherited con 67 stitution of the bird. In comparing the behaviour of the migratory male with that of the resident, attention was drawn to the manner in which the occupation of a territory was effected: the former bird, it may be remembered, established itself without delay, whereas the latter did so only by degrees, and the difference was attributed to the incidence of migration which required a closer correspondence between organic process and external environment. But the significance for us just now lies in the fact that the definiteness, which accompanies the initial behaviour of the migratory male in relation to the territory, cannot have been acquired by repetition; for this reason, that when the male occupies its space of ground at the end of its long and arduous journey, it does so without preparation or experiment, even without hesitation, as if aware that it was making good the first step in the process of reproduction. No doubt, if it happened to be an individual that had already experienced the enjoyment of reproduction, it might be aware of the immediate results to be achieved and act accordingly. But among the hosts of migrants that one observes, there must be many males which have not previously mated; and yet, upon arrival, they all behave in a similarly definite manner—so that experience cannot well be the primary factor in the situation. If, then, the essential condition of habit formation is absent and experience is eliminated, there is nothing left but racial preparation to fall back upon.

68 Nevertheless, it is true that many

resident males seem to pass through a period of indecision before they establish themselves permanently in their respective territories; they come and go, their visits grow more and more prolonged, and only after the lapse of some considerable time does the process of establishment attain that degree of completeness which is represented in the initial behaviour of the migratory male. Their whole procedure seems therefore to bear the stamp of individual acquirement; and, if it stood alone, we might be content to construe it thus, but the example of the migratory male necessitates our looking elsewhere for the real meaning of the indecision.

Let me first of all give some instances of the persistence with which a male remains in one spot, and this despite the fact that it has no mate.

A Reed-Bunting occupied a central territory in a strip of marshy ground inhabited annually by four or five males of this species. Throughout April, May, and until the 19th June, it clung to its small plot of ground, tolerated no intrusion, and sang incessantly.

Two Whitethroats arrived at much the same time—the 30th April approximately—and occupied the corner of a small plantation; the one obtained a mate the day following its arrival, the other remained unpaired for a fortnight.

A Reed-Warbler established itself amongst 69 some willows and alders adjoining a reed-bed and made its headquarters in a small willow bush. Not more than fifteen yards away, on the edge of the main portion of the reeds, another male was established and was paired on the 22nd May. Each morning the single male behaved in much the same way, singing continuously whilst perched upon the bush. And so the days passed by until it seemed improbable that it would ever secure a mate, but one appeared on the 20th June, and a nest was built forthwith.

Now it is difficult to believe that a chance visit, even though repeated for a few mornings in succession, could have accounted for the Reed-Bunting remaining so persistently in the marsh, or the Whitethroat in one corner of the osier bed, or the Reed-Warbler in that one particular willow. Not only so, but if a habit of such evident strength can be acquired so readily, we have a right to ask why it should only be acquired in the spring—why not at every season? Considerations such as these lead to the belief that there must be some congenital basis to account for such persistent endeavour; the more so since it is difficult not to be impressed with the conative aspect of the male's behaviour. To a stranger, unacquainted with its previous history, the bird might appear to be leading a life of hesitation, whereas, if carefully watched, its whole attitude will be found to betray symptoms of a striving towards some end; and the frequent departure and return, which might 70 be pointed to as the material from which a definite mode of procedure would be likely to emerge, is in reality behaviour of a determinate sort.

My interpretation, then, of the apparent indecision in the behaviour of the resident male is this. During the winter most species live in societies, together they seek their food and together they retire in the evening to the accustomed roosting places, and the association of different individuals confers mutual benefits upon the associates. The movements of these societies are dominated by the question of food; all else is subservient, and the supply of the necessary sustenance may, under certain conditions, become a difficulty which can only be met by energy and resource. After the long night the sensation of hunger is strong, and the birds, on awakening, fly to the accustomed feeding grounds, returning again in the evening to the selected spot, and by frequent repetition a routine becomes established. Thus the behaviour of each individual is determined not only by the powerful gregarious impulse but also by the habits formed in connection therewith during many weeks in succession. Now with the rise of the appropriate organic state, the disposition to seek the breeding ground and there to establish itself becomes dominant in the male. But the process is a gradual one. There is no need, as happens amongst the migrants, for the period of organic change to conform rigidly to the growth of 71 any particular condition in the environment, and hence for a time the bird oscillates between two modes of behaviour—between that one organised by frequent repetition and that one determined by the functioning of this new disposition.

To look at the matter broadly, it is scarcely likely that so definite a mode of behaviour would recur with such regularity, generation after generation, in the individuals belonging to so many widely divergent forms, if it had no root in the inborn constitution of the bird. But the law of habit formation has its part to play also. By itself it is inadequate; yet it probably does assist very materially in adding still greater definition, and it probably is responsible in a large measure for determining the limits of the territory according to the conditions of existence of the species—thus the Falcon seeks its prey over wide tracts of land, and, by hunting over certain ground repeatedly, establishes a routine, which broadly fixes the area occupied; the Woodpecker cannot find food upon every tree, and every forest does not contain the necessary trees, and therefore the bird regulates its flight according to the position of the trees; and the Warbler, finding food close at hand, does not need to travel far, and the area it occupies is consequently small.

So that the most likely solution of the problem will be found in a combination of our second and third propositions; that is to say, in 72 an initial responsive behaviour provided for in the inherited constitution of the nervous system, and in a definiteness acquired by repetition and determined by relationships in the external environment.
72

CHAPTER III

THE DISPOSITION TO DEFEND THE TERRITORY

In the previous chapter I endeavoured to show that each male establishes a territory at the commencement of the breeding season, and there isolates itself from members of its own sex. And further I gave my reasons for believing that this particular mode of behaviour is determined by the inherited nature of the bird, and that we are justified in speaking of it as "a disposition to secure a territory" because we can perceive its prospective value. But the act of establishment is only one step towards "securing." By itself it can achieve nothing; for any number of different individuals might fix upon the same situation, and if there were nothing in the inherited constitution of the bird to prevent this happening, where would be the security, or how could any benefit accrue to the species?

In withdrawing from its companions in the spring, the male is breaking with the past, and this action marks a definite change in its routine of existence. But the change does not end in attempted isolation; it is carried farther and extends to the innermost life and affects what, 74 humanly speaking, we should term its emotional nature, so that the bird becomes openly hostile towards other males with whom previously it had lived on amicable terms.

The seasonal organic condition is responsible for the functioning of the disposition which results in this intolerance, just as it is for the functioning of the disposition which leads to the establishment of the territory; and the effect of these two dispositions is that a space of ground is not only occupied but made secure from intrusion. The process is a simple one. There is no reason to believe, there is no necessity to believe, that any part of the procedure is conditioned by anticipatory meaning; the behaviour is "instinctive" in Professor Lloyd Morgan's definition of the word, since it is of a "specific congenital type, dependent upon purely biological conditions, nowise guided by conscious experience though affording data for the life of consciousness."

That the males of many animals are apt to become quarrelsome during the mating period is notorious. Darwin collected a number of facts, many of which related to birds, showing the nature and extent of the strife when the sexual instinct dominated the situation. And pondering over these facts, he deduced therefrom a "law of battle," which, he believed, bore a direct relation to the possession of a female. And it must be admitted that he had excellent ground for his conclusion in the fact not only that the conflicts occur mainly during the pairing season, but that 75 the female is often a spectator and seems even to pair with the victor. I accepted it, therefore, as the most reasonable interpretation of the facts. But, as time passed by, incidents of a conflicting character led me to think that after all there might be another solution of the problem. And when it was no longer possible to doubt that there was a widespread tendency to establish territories, it at once became manifest that the battles might have an important part to play in the whole scheme. But how was this to be proved? What sort of evidence could show whether the proximate end for which the males were fighting had reference to the female or to the territory? Clearly nothing but a complete record of the whole series of events leading up to reproduction could supply the necessary data upon which a decision might rest. In the present chapter I shall give, in the first place, the reasons which lead me to think that the origin of the fighting cannot be traced to the female; afterwards, the evidence which seems to show that it must be sought in the territory; and finally, I shall make a suggestion as to the part the female may play in the whole scheme.

Male Blackbirds fighting for the possession of territory. The bare skin on the crown of the defeated bird shows the nature of the injuries from which it succumbed.

The facts upon which the "law of battle" was founded were ample to establish the truth of its main doctrine. But the evidence upon which the interpretation of the battles was based was somewhat superficial. It was based mainly upon the general observation that one or more females could frequently be observed to accompany the combatants; and if this were the sole condition 76 under which the fighting occurred, one must admit that this view would have much to recommend it. But it is not merely a question of males disputing in the presence of a female; for males fight when no female is present, pair attacks pair, or a male may even attack a female—in fact there is a complexity of strife which is bewildering.

In attributing the rivalry to the presence of the female, it is assumed that males are in a preponderance, and that consequently two or more are always ready to compete for a mate. Her presence is presumably the condition under which his pugnacious nature is rendered susceptible to its appropriate stimulus, the stimulus being, of course, supplied by the opponent. There would be nothing against this interpretation if it were in accord with the facts; but it can, I think, be shown that the males are just as pugnacious and the conflicts just as severe even when the question of securing a mate is definitely excluded; and I shall now give the evidence which has led me to this conclusion.

In the previous chapter we had occasion to refer to the difference in the times of arrival of the male and female migrants, and we came to the conclusion, it may be remembered, that this was a fact of some importance, because it gave us a clue to the meaning of much that was otherwise obscure in their behaviour. But it is also of importance in connection with the particular aspect of the problem which we now have in view, for if it 77 can be shown that males, when they first reach their breeding grounds, are even then intolerant of one another's presence, if their actions and attitudes betray similar symptoms of quasi-conation, if disputes are rife and the struggles of a kind to preclude all doubt as to their reality, then it is manifest that in such cases their intolerance cannot be due to the presence of the female.

Here, however, I must refer to a view which is held by some psychologists, namely, that amongst the higher animals, even on the occasion of the first performance of an instinctive act, there is some vague awareness of the proximate end to be attained. Discussing the nature of instincts, Dr M'Dougall 3 says, "Nor does our definition insist, as some do, that the instinctive action is performed without awareness of the end towards which it tends, for this, too, is not essential; it may be, and in the case of the lower animals no doubt often is, so performed, as also by the very young child, but in the case of the higher animals some prevision of the immediate end, however vague, probably accompanies an instinctive action that has often been repeated." A similar view seems to be held by Dr Stout. 4 "As I have already shown," he says, "animals in their instinctive actions do actually behave from the outset as if they were continuously interested in the development of what is for them one and the same situation or course of events; they actually 78 behave as if they were continuously attentive, looking forward beyond the immediately present experience in preparation for what is to come. They apparently watch, wait, search, are on the alert. They also behave exactly as if they appreciated a difference between relative success and failure, trying again when a certain perceptible result is not attained and varying their procedure in so far as it has been unsuccessful. All these characters are found in the first nest-building of birds as well as in the second; they are found also in courses of conduct which occur only once in the lifetime of the animal." Both these writers would, I imagine, contend that, even when a female is absent, the idea of the female, as the end in view throughout, is present; and they would argue that the fact of her absence during the fighting in no way disposes of the belief that she is the condition under which the pugnacious instinct of the male is rendered susceptible to stimulation. What reason is there to think that this interpretation is applicable to the case under consideration? When a female is present, we observe that the males are pugnacious, and, when she is absent, that they still continue to be hostile—that is to say, they behave *as if* she were present. Now, as far as I can ascertain, the "*as if*" is the only ground there is for supposing that the female is represented in imaginal form—there is no evidence of the fact, if fact it be. On the contrary, the behaviour of the male affords some fairly conclusive evidence 79 that no such image is the primary factor in exciting the instinctive reaction. For if it be the actual presence of the female, or, in the absence of such, a mental image, that renders the pugnacious nature of the male responsive; provided the usual stimulus were present, the instinct ought surely to respond, not only under one particular circumstance, but under all circumstances. Yet, as we shall presently see, a male is by no means consistently intolerant of other males. It may be sociable at one moment or pugnacious at another, but the pugnacity is always peculiar to a certain occasion—the occupation of a territory. What shall we say then—that a mental image is a situational item only when the territory is occupied? It may be so; it may be that the fact of occupation gives rise to the mental image which, in its turn, renders the fighting instinct explosive, which again renders the possession of the territory secure. That such an interpretation is possible we must all admit. But if it were true, though it would not affect the main consideration, namely, whether the fighting has reference to the possession of a particular female, or to the protection of the territory, it would make further discussion as to which of these is the condition of the fighting unprofitable, for each would have its part to play in the process, the territory remaining, however, the principal factor in the situation.

Now the difference in the times of arrival of the male and female migrant varies in 80 different species from a few days to a fortnight or even more. It is most marked in those that return to their breeding grounds early in the season, and the greater the margin of difference the greater scope is there for observation. In my records for the past twelve years, there are frequent references to these initial male contests in the life of the Willow-Warbler and of the Chiffchaff; and in the district which I have in mind, these two species arrive early in the season, the males preceding the females by a week or even as much as a fortnight. Suppose, then, that two Chiffchaffs establish themselves in adjoining territories; or suppose that a male settles in a territory already occupied; what is the result? Well, scenes of hostility soon become apparent; as the birds approach one another they become more and more restive, their song ceases, they no longer search for food in the usual methodical manner, but instead their movements are hurried and their call-notes are uttered rapidly—all of which betrays a heightened emotional tone. Then the climax is reached, there is a momentary fluttering of tiny wings, a clicking of bills, and for the time being that may be all. But unless one or other of the combatants retires, this scene may be repeated many times in the course of a few hours, and repeated with varying degrees of severity. Yet the fighting, even in the most extreme form, when the birds locked together fall slowly to the ground, is seldom of an impressive kind, and one has to bear in mind the capabilities of the actors, remembering that 81 the most severe struggle might readily be interpreted as a game if it were not for certain symptoms which reveal its inner nature.

The males of many other migrants can frequently be observed to fight when there was every reason to believe that females had still to arrive. The Blackcap is notoriously pugnacious, but not more so than the Marsh-Warbler or the Whinchat. Here in Worcestershire, the *Arundo phragmites* grows mainly on certain sheets of water which are comparatively few and far between, and the Reed-Warbler is consequently restricted to isolated and more or less confined areas. The males arrive early in May before the new growth of reeds has attained any considerable height, and each one has its own position in the reed-bed, sings there, and throughout the whole period of reproduction actively resists intrusion on the part of other males. I have kept watch upon a small area of reeds daily from the date of the first arrival; each individual was known to me, and as the growing reeds were only a few inches in height, a female could scarcely have escaped detection. Yet time and again disputes arose, and males pursued and pecked one another, striving to attain that isolation for which racial preparation had fitted them.

But on account of their violence, or their novelty, or because the absence of a female was beyond question, some battles stand out in one's memory more prominently than others. An instance of this was a struggle between two 82 Whitethroats which happened in the latter part of April and lasted for three successive days. The scene of its occurrence was more or less the same on each occasion, and the area over which the birds wandered was comparatively small. The fighting was characterised by persistent effort and was of a most determined kind, and so engrossed did the assailants become that they even fluttered to the ground at my feet. No trace of a female was to be seen at any time during these three days, nor, during the pauses in the conflict, was the emotional behaviour of a kind which led me to suppose that a female was anywhere in the vicinity. And, if she had been near, she must have made her presence known, for the belief that she is a timid creature, skulking on such occasions in the undergrowth, is by no means borne out by experience.

Even more impressive was a battle between two male Cuckoos. It occurred high up in the air above the tops of some tall elm-trees which roughly marked the boundary line between their respective areas, and the actions of the birds were plainly visible. At the moment of actual collision the opponents were generally in a vertical position, and wings, feet, and beaks were made use of in turn; one could plainly see them strike at one another with their feet, and one could observe the open bill which generally denotes exhaustion, but may of course have been due to anger, or used as a means of producing terror. Yet no female appeared in the locality until six days after the occurrence of this struggle—and 83 she certainly is not easily overlooked, for her note is unmistakable even when the behaviour of the male does not betray her arrival.

Male Cuckoos fighting before the arrival of a female

That the actual presence of the respective females exercised any influence on the course of these struggles is more than doubtful. Not only did one fail to detect them, but one's failure to do so was confirmed by the knowledge that they had not yet arrived in those particular localities. Hence the fact of the male preceding the female is a valuable aid to the interpretation of subsequent behaviour; and one appreciates it the more after having experienced the difficulty of deciding whether she is present during the conflicts between resident males, for no matter how carefully we may observe the conditions which lead up to, and which accompany, such conflicts, or how closely we may scrutinise the surrounding trees, undergrowth, or ground, there always remains the possibility that she may, after all, have been overlooked. But this must not be taken to imply that in such cases direct observation alone can lead to no serviceable result, or that the evidence gained therefrom is worthless. Far from it. Failure to detect a female is so very common an occurrence that, even if we lacked the corroborative evidence supplied in the life of the migratory male, it would still be unreasonable to suppose that it were solely due to mistaken observation. We mark her absence during the conflicts between the respective males of many common species—the Finches, Buntings, and Thrushes that occupy 84 their territories early in the season when the hedgerows and trees are still bare; but more frequently amongst those that inhabit open ground, because the movements of the birds are there more accessible to observation. For instance, half a dozen or more Lapwings can be kept in view at the same time, and as they stand at dawn in solitary state, keeping watch upon their respective territories, they are conspicuous objects on the short, frosted grass; no stranger can enter the arena without the observer being aware of it, no commotion can occur but one detects it, no movement however small need be missed. And so they fight, in a manner which leaves no doubt as to the reality of the struggle, when their prospective mates are absent not only from the particular territories in which the conflicts take place, but absent too from those adjoining.

If the fact that males fight before they are paired and in the absence of a female could be placed beyond all question, it would no longer be possible to regard her possession as the end for which they are contending, and consequently there would be no need to produce further evidence. But the examples which I have given refer, of course, to only a few migrants and a few residents—and moreover it must be admitted that a female *is* often conspicuous during the battles—so that by themselves they must be regarded, and rightly so, as inconclusive. We must therefore pass on to consider evidence of a somewhat different character.

I spoke of the complexity of the strife. By 85 this I mean that it is not merely a matter of disputes between adjoining males, but that it is a far more comprehensive business involving both sexes. Thus female fights with female and pair with pair, or a male will attack a female, or, again, a pair will combine against a single male or a single female. And from all this complexity of strife we gain much valuable evidence in regard to the question immediately before us. For when one pair attacks another, or males that are definitely paired fight with one another, or an unpaired male attacks either sex of a neighbouring pair indiscriminately, there is surely little ground for supposing that the possession of a mate is the reason of it all.

The battles between pairs of the same species are by no means uncommon. Observe, for example, the central pair of three pairs of Reed-Buntings occupying adjoining territories, and keep a daily record of the routine of activity practised by both sexes during the early hours of the morning; then, at the close of the season, summarise all the fighting under different headings, and it will be found that the number of occasions upon which the central pair attacked, or was attacked by, neighbouring pairs will form a considerable portion of the whole.

Or watch the Moor-Hen, and for the purpose choose some sheet of water large enough to accommodate three or more pairs, and so situated that the birds can always be kept in view. Early in February the pool will be haunted by numbers of individuals of both sexes, all 86 swimming about together, and, if the pool is surrounded by arable land, wandering over that land subject to no territorial restrictions, apparently free to seek food where they will. But as time goes by, their number gradually decreases until a few pairs only remain, and these will occupy definite areas. If careful watch is then kept and the relations of the pairs closely studied, there will be no difficulty in observing the particular kind of warfare to which I am alluding, and it will be noticed that the encounters are of a particularly violent description. Thus two pairs approach one another, and, when they meet, throw themselves upon their backs, each bird striking at its adversary with its feet or seizing hold of it with its beak; and though, in the commotion that ensues, it is almost impossible to determine what exactly is happening, there is reason to believe that the sexes attack one another indiscriminately.

A struggle between two pairs of Pied Wagtails is worth mentioning. It impressed itself upon my memory because of the unusual vigour with which it was conducted. The battle lasted for fifteen minutes or more, and the four birds, collecting together, pursued and attacked one another—at one moment in the air, at another upon the roof of a house where they would alight and flutter about on the slates, uttering their call-note without ceasing—until finally they disappeared from view, still, however, continuing the struggle.

Two pairs of Pied Wagtails fighting in defence of their territories.

Such is the nature of the warfare which 87 prevails between neighbouring pairs, and which can be observed in the life of many other species—the Chaffinch, Stonechat, Blackbird, Partridge, Jay, to mention but a few.

The conflicts between males that are definitely paired are of such common occurrence that it is scarcely necessary to mention specific instances. But the occasions on which a male attacks either sex of a neighbouring pair indiscriminately, or on which a pair combine to attack a female, are less frequent.

Now if it be true that males fight for no other purpose than to gain possession of a mate, what meaning are we to attach to the battles between the pairs, or what explanation are we to give of the fact that paired males are so frequently hostile? Those who hold this view will probably argue thus: "The presence of the female is the condition under which the pugnacious instinct of the male is rendered susceptible to appropriate stimulation, and the stimulus is supplied by a rival male; we admit that all the fighting which occurs after pairing has taken place has nothing to do strictly speaking with gaining a mate, but, inasmuch as the fact of possession is always liable to be challenged—and no male can differentiate between a paired and an unpaired intruder—we contend that it would add to the security of possession if the pugnacious instinct remained susceptible to stimulation so long as there were any possibility of challenge from an unpaired male; and we think that the waste of energy involved in 88 the struggles between paired birds, and which we grant is purposeless, would be more than balanced by the added security." This is a possible explanation and requires consideration. It cannot account for all the diverse ways in which the sexes are mixed up in the fighting—it cannot, for instance, explain the fact that an unpaired male will attack either sex of an adjoining pair indiscriminately—but nevertheless it appears at first sight to be a reasonable explanation of some of them. We must remember, however, that fighting continues throughout the whole period of reproduction. Even after the discharge of the sexual function has ceased, and the female is engaged in incubation or in tending her young, the male is still intolerant of intruders; and it is difficult to believe that, at so late a stage in the process, a female could be any attraction sexually to an unpaired male. But apart from any theoretical objection, there remains the fact—namely that there is no evidence that a male, after having once paired, is liable to be robbed of its mate. And in support of this fact I have only to state that I have met with no single instance of failure to obtain and hold a mate when once a territory had been secured. Bearing in mind then that both sexes participate in the fighting, and that individuals of the opposite sex frequently attack one another; that all such conflicts are characterised by persistent effort, and that they are not limited to just the particular period when the sexual instinct is 89 dominant but continue throughout the breeding season; bearing in mind that in at least one form of this promiscuous warfare the influence of the female can be definitely excluded, and that, in the remaining forms, the evidence which is required to link them up with the biological end of securing mates is lacking—can it be denied that the complexity of the strife makes against the view that the possession of a female is the proximate end for which the males are fighting?

We started with the most simple aspect of the whole problem, the fighting of two males in the presence of one female—the aspect upon which attention has usually been fixed. And if it remained at that, if observation failed to disclose any further development in the situation, then there would be no need to probe the matter deeper, there would be no reason to doubt the assertion that the quarrel had direct reference to the female. But assuredly no one can ponder over the diversity of battle and still believe that the possession of a mate furnishes an adequate solution of the mystery. Clearly such an hypothesis cannot cover all the known facts; there are conflicts between separate pairs, and there are conflicts between males when females are known to be absent and when their mates are even engaged in the work of incubation—these cannot be due to an impulse in a member of one sex to gain or keep possession of one of the other sex. So that taking all these facts into consideration, we are 90 justified, I think, in hesitating to accept this view, and must look elsewhere for the real condition under which the pugnacious nature of the male is rendered susceptible to appropriate stimulation.

What then is the meaning of all this warfare? The process of reproduction is a complex one, built up of a number of different parts forming one inter-related whole; it is not merely a question of "battle," or of "territory," or of "song," or of "emotional manifestation," but of all these together. The fighting is thus one link in a chain of events whose end is the attainment of reproduction; it is a relationship in an inter-related process, and to speak of it as being even directly related to the territory is scarcely sufficient, for it is intimately associated with the disposition which is manifested in the isolation of the male from its companions, and forms therewith an *imperium in imperio* from which our concept of breeding territory is taken. But let me say at once that it is no easy matter to prove this, for since so many modes of behaviour, which can be interpreted as lending support to this view, are likewise interpretable on the view that the presence of a female is a necessary condition of the fighting, it is difficult to find just the sort of evidence that is required. Nevertheless, after hearing the whole of the evidence and at the same time keeping in mind the conclusion which we have already reached, I venture to 91 think that the close relationship between the warfare on the one hand and the territory on the other will be fully admitted.

Formerly I deemed the spring rivalry to be the result of accidental encounters, and I believed that an issue to a struggle was only reached when one of the combatants succumbed or disappeared from the locality, a view which neither recognised method nor admitted control. Recent experience has shown, however, that I was wrong, and that there is a very definite control over and above that which is supplied by the physical capabilities of the birds.

Let us take some common species, the Willow-Warbler being our first example; and, having found three adjoining territories occupied by unpaired males, let us study the conflicts at each stage in the sexual life of the three individuals, observing them before females have arrived upon the scene, again when one or two of the three males have secured mates, and yet again when all three have paired. Now we shall find that the conditions which lead up to and which terminate the conflicts are remarkably alike at each of these periods. A male intrudes, and the intrusion evokes an immediate display of irritation on the part of the owner of the territory, who, rapidly uttering its song and jerking its wings, begins hostilities. Flying towards the intruder, it attacks viciously, and there follows much fluttering of wings and snapping or clicking of bills. At one moment the birds are in the tree-tops, at another in the 92 air, and sometimes even on the ground, and fighting thus they gradually approach and pass beyond the limits of the territory. Whereupon a change comes over the scene; the male whose territory was intruded upon and who all along had displayed such animosity, betrays no further interest in the conflict—it ceases to attack, searches around for food, or sings, and slowly makes its way back towards the centre of the territory.

Scenes of this kind are of almost daily occurrence wherever a species is so common, or the environment to which it is adapted so limited in extent, that males are obliged to occupy adjacent ground. The Moor-Hen abounds on all suitable sheets of water, and it is a bird that can be conveniently studied because, as a rule, there is nothing, except the rushes that fringe the pool, to hinder us from obtaining a panoramic view of the whole proceedings, and moreover the area occupied by each individual is comparatively small. Towards the middle of February, symptoms of sexual organic change make themselves apparent, and the pool is then no longer the resort of a peaceable community; quarrels become frequent, and as different portions of the surface of the water are gradually appropriated, so the fighting becomes more incessant and more severe. Each individual has its own particular territory, embracing a piece of open water as well as a part of the rush-covered fringe, within which it moves and lives. But in the early part of the season, when the 93 territories are still in process of being established, and definiteness has still to be acquired, trespassing is of frequent occurrence, and the conflicts are often conspicuous for their severity.

Now these conflicts are not confined to unpaired individuals, nor to one sex, nor to one member of a pair—every individual that has settled upon the pool for the purpose of breeding will at one time or another be involved in a struggle with its neighbour. If then we single out certain pairs and day by day observe their actions and their attitude towards intruders, we shall notice that, instead of their routine of existence consisting, as a casual acquaintance with the pool and its inmates might lead us to believe, of an endless series of meaningless disputes, the behaviour of each individual is directed towards a similar goal—the increasing of the security of its possession; and further, if we pay particular attention to the circumstances which lead up to the quarrels and the circumstances under which such quarrels come to an end, we shall find, when we have accumulated a sufficient body of observations, that the disputes always originate in trespass, and that hostilities always cease when the trespasser returns again to its own territory. By careful observation it is possible to make oneself acquainted with the boundaries—I know not what other term to use—which separate this territory from that; and it is the conduct of the birds on or near these boundaries to which attention must be drawn. A bird may be 94 feeding quietly in one corner of its territory when an intruder enters. Becoming aware of what is happening it ceases to search for food, and approaching the intruder, at first swimming slowly but gradually increasing its pace, it finally rises and attacks with wings and beak, and drives its rival back again beyond the boundary. Thereupon its attitude undergoes a remarkable change; ceasing to attack, but remaining standing for a few moments as if still keeping guard, it betrays no further interest in the bird with which a few seconds previously it was fighting furiously. On one occasion I watched a trespasser settle upon a conspicuous clump of rushes situated near the boundary. The owner, who was at the moment some distance away, approached in the usual manner, and, having driven off the trespasser, returned immediately to the clump, where it remained erect and motionless.

A feature which marks all the fighting, and which we cannot afford to disregard, is the conative aspect of the behaviour of the owner of the territory. The bird attacks with apparent deliberation *as if* it were striving to attain some definite end. I recollect an incident which was interesting from this point of view. A pair of Reed-Buntings were disturbed by a Weasel which had approached their nest containing young. Both birds betrayed symptoms of excitement; as the Weasel threaded its way amongst the rushes, so they fluttered from clump to clump or clung to the stems, uttering 95 a note which is peculiar to times of distress, and followed it thus until finally it disappeared in a hedge. The rapidly uttered note and the excitement of the birds caused some commotion, and the male from an adjoining territory approached the scene. Now one would have expected that the presence of this bird, and possibly its aid in driving away a common enemy, would have been welcomed; one would have thought that all else would have been subservient to the common danger, and that so real a menace to the offspring would have evoked an impulse in the parent powerful enough to dominate the situation and subordinate all the activities of the bird to the attainment of its end. But what happened? Three times during this incident, the male, whose young were in danger, abandoned the pursuit of the Weasel and pursued the intruder. It was not merely that he objected to the presence of this neighbouring male in a passive way, nor even that he had a momentary skirmish with it, but that he determinedly drove the intruder beyond the boundary and only then returned to harass the Weasel.

Thus it seems clear that the proximate end to which the fighting is directed is not necessarily the defeat of the intruder, but its removal from a certain position. And inasmuch as this result will be obtained whether the retreat is brought about by fear of an opponent or by physical exhaustion, it is manifest that too much significance need not be attached to the amount of 96 injury inflicted. It is necessary to bear this in mind, because it is held by some, who have carefully observed the actions of various species, that overmuch importance is attached to the conflicts, that in a large number of instances they are mere "bickerings" and lead to nothing, and that they are now only "formal," which means, I suppose, that they are vestigial—fragments of warfare that determined the survival of the species in bygone ages. But if the conclusion at which we have just arrived be correct, if we can recognise a single aim passing through the whole of the warfare—and that one the removal of an intruder from a certain position, then we need no longer concern ourselves as to the degree of severity of the battles—we see it all in true perspective. Neither exhaustion nor physical inability are the sole factors which determine the nature and extent of the fighting; there is a more important factor still—position. According, that is to say, to the position which a bird occupies whilst fighting is in progress, so its pugnacious nature gains or loses susceptibility, and it is this gain or loss of susceptibility which I refer to when I speak of the fighting as being controlled.

What we have then to consider is the relation of "susceptibility" to "position." We can explain the relationship in two ways. We can say that the part of the nature of the male which leads to the occupation of a territory, and is partly hereditary and partly acquired, is stronger than the part which leads the bird to fight, and 97 which is conditioned by the presence of a female, and that consequently when the male passes the boundary, the impulse to return asserts itself and the conflict ceases; or we can say that the occupation of a territory is the condition under which the pugnacious instinct is rendered susceptible to stimulation, that the stimulus is supplied by the intruder, and that when the male passes outside the accustomed area its instinct is no longer so susceptible and it therefore retires from the conflict.

Of these explanations, the first is not altogether satisfactory. It requires the presence of a female and, as we have

Long-tailed Tit
Males fighting for the possession of territory. The feathers have been torn from the crown of the defeated and dying rival

seen, a female is by no means always present. Then it attributes to the one side of the inherited nature an influence which is not borne out by the facts, for in the ordinary routine of existence, without the incentive of battle, every individual is liable to wander occasionally beyond its boundary and to intrude temporarily upon its neighbours; and this it could scarcely do, providing its nature to remain within the territory were powerful enough to dominate its movements and curtail its activities even during the excitement of an encounter. But there is nothing inherently improbable in the alternative hypothesis, nor anything that is at all inconsistent with the behaviour as observed; on the contrary, if it is admitted, the facts become connected together and exhibit a meaning which they otherwise would not have possessed.

So much for the controlling influence of 98 "position," which alone seems to me sufficient ground for believing that the fighting has reference to the territory. But it is not the whole of the evidence.

Now if it were possible to demonstrate by actual observation that those males which had not established territories were not pugnacious, we should have something in the nature of proof of the correctness of this view. Demonstrative evidence of this kind is, however, unattainable. Yet we can come very near to obtaining it by reason of a peculiar feature which marks the process of acquiring territory—the neutral ground. The Lapwing will serve as an illustration. In the previous chapter I referred to the small flocks that appeared in the accustomed water meadow early in February, and I described how they settled day after day in that meadow, but only in a limited part of it, where they passed their time in rest, in preening their feathers, or in running this way and that lazily searching for food; and how, at length, the flock dwindled by reason of individuals breaking away in order to secure positions on the remaining part of the meadow. Here the neutral ground is adjacent to the territories, and, while still occupied by the flock, is resorted to by the males that had deserted that flock in order to establish those territories.

Suppose now that we have the whole meadow in view from some point of vantage. In front of us are the territories, in the distance the neutral ground; and in each territory there 99 is a solitary male, while on the neutral ground a number of individuals of both sexes are assembled, and move about freely one amongst another. So that the scene presented to view is somewhat as follows: a flat meadow, at one end of which, and at fairly regular intervals, a few solitary individuals are dotted about, each one keeping at a distance from its neighbours; while at the other end a number of individuals are collected together in a comparatively small space, apparently deriving some satisfaction from their close association. That surely is a very remarkable contrast. But let us continue our investigation, first fixing our attention upon the solitary individuals; one is standing preening its feathers, another is squatting upon the ground, a third runs a few yards in this direction then a few yards in that, stimulated apparently by the sight of food, and so on. Moreover, each one keeps strictly to a well-defined area and makes no attempt to associate with its fellows. One of the males, however, whilst roaming backwards and forwards approaches the limit of its territory, and this brings the neighbouring bird, whose boundary is threatened, rapidly to the spot. In an upright position both stand face to face, and the battle then begins; with their wings they attempt to beat one another about the body, with their beaks they aim blows at the head, and in the mêlée wings and legs seem to be inextricably mixed; whilst at intervals, driven backwards by the force of the collision, they are compelled to separate, only, however, to return to 100 the charge—and the sound of beating wings and the feathers that float in the air are tokens of earnestness. Such scenes are of frequent occurrence; but the conflicts vary in intensity, and the circumstances under which they occur vary too, and females come and go without leaving any clue as to their ultimate intentions.

Turning now to the flock one is impressed with the friendship that seems to exist between the various members. There are, it is true, occasional displays of pugnacity which never seem to develop into anything very serious; for instance, one bird will fly at another, and a momentary scuffle is followed by a short pursuit but nothing more—nothing, that is to say, in the least comparable with the battle previously described. Of what is the flock composed? Of members of both sexes. There is no difficulty in assuring oneself that this is so. But is it entirely composed of individuals in whom development has not reached a stage adequate for the functioning of the primary dispositions? No, not entirely; for it will be observed that its number is a fluctuating one, that birds come and go, and, if a close watch is kept upon the different individuals as they leave, it will be noticed that some at least are inmates of the territories at the opposite end of the meadow—the solitary members whose behaviour we were recently watching. This fact is an important one. We were impressed, it may be remembered, with the contrast between the general behaviour of the birds at the opposite ends of the meadow. 101 But now it appears as if the contrast were not between this individual and that, but between the behaviour of the same one under different circumstances. The male, that is to say, which, while in its territory, tolerates the approach of no other male, flies to the flock and is there welcomed by the very individuals with whom a short time previously it had been engaged in serious conflict.

But if the conditions are reversed and the flock happens to settle in an occupied territory, the attitude of the owner towards the flock is very different. In the year 1916 an incident of this kind occurred in the meadow to which reference has already been made. The weather had been exceptionally severe—very cold easterly and north-easterly winds, frost, and frequent falls of snow had affected the behaviour of the Lapwings, and seemed to have checked the normal development of their sexual routine. The males would attempt to establish themselves, and then, when the temperature fell and the ground was covered with snow, would collect again in flocks and follow their winter routine. It was on the 9th March, during one of the spells of milder weather, that the flock on the neutral ground was disturbed and settled mainly in the territory marked No. 3 on the 1916 plan, but partly on that marked No. 2. The owners thereupon began to attack the different members of the invading flock. Fixing attention upon a particular bird whilst ignoring the remainder, the No. 3 male drove it away, and then after 102 a pause drove another away, and so on until by degrees all the invaders were banished, and the No. 2 male did likewise. The interest of this incident lies, however, in the behaviour of the different individuals of which the flock was composed; when attacked they made no real show of resistance, but accepted the situation and left. The will to fight was clearly lacking, yet their presence was a source of annoyance to the owners of the territories. A short time previously a female had accompanied one of the males and was at that time somewhere in the vicinity, but beyond this there was no evidence to show that either of them were paired, and even if the presence of the female were the reason of the pugnacity of the one, it could not well account for that of the other.

The neutral ground does not always happen to be so close at hand as in the case of the meadow referred to. Sometimes the birds will resort to a particular field, attracted probably by a plentiful supply of food, and here they collect and behave as they do during the winter, running this way and that as the fancy takes them, meeting together by accident at one moment, parting at another, according to the direction in which they happen to wander. Of animosity there is little sign; the season might be the middle of winter instead of the middle of March for all the indication there is of sexual development, and yet one knows that they will behave differently when they 103 leave this ground, as presently they will, and return to their territories in the surrounding neighbourhood, and that there each one will fight if necessary to preserve its acre from intrusion.

It would seem, then, from this that the fighting must bear some relation to the particular area of ground in which it occurs; and unless it can be shown that there is some other factor in the external environment of the male, that is the direction in which we must look for the condition under which the instinct is rendered susceptible. One's thoughts turn, of course, to the female, but she too passes backwards and forwards between the territories and the neutral ground, and if her presence were really a *conditio sine qua non* of the strife, one would like to know why, when she leaves those territories and joins the flock and the males do likewise, similar conflicts should not prevail there also.

Other species have their neutral ground, but the environment seldom affords such facilities for observation as does that of the Lapwing. Even though the Moor-Hens, who are so conspicuously intolerant upon the pool, *do* feed together amicably upon the meadows adjoining; and the Chaffinch that is so pugnacious in the morning, *does* seek out the flock later in the day; yet their conditions of existence prevent our obtaining a panoramic view of the whole proceeding, and we have to study each scene separately before discovering that the relation 104 ship between intolerance and the territory on the one hand, and friendship and the neutral ground on the other, is just as strong a feature as it is in the behaviour of the Lapwing.

I shall now give a brief account of the conduct of a male Reed-Bunting which by persistent effort established itself late in the season, and I shall do so because its behaviour tends to confirm much that has been said in the preceding pages.

Early in March three male Reed-Buntings occupied a small water meadow overgrown with the common rush, and by the third week all of them were paired. On the 30th March two of the males were unusually pugnacious, and on the following day fighting continued and at times was very severe. Now I knew that the occupants of the ground in which the fighting was taking place were paired, and not doubting that the combatants were the owners of two territories marked for convenience sake Nos. 1 and 2, I was at a loss to understand the meaning of so determined and persistent a struggle. My attention, however, was presently drawn to a third bird, which also joined in the conflict and made the whole situation still more perplexing. This bird, as it soon became clear, was none other than the owner of No. 2 territory, and the one that I had previously regarded as such was a new arrival. On the following day, the 1st April, fighting continued, and in my record for that 105 day there is a note to the effect that "No. 2 female seems to be of no interest to No. 5 male (the new arrival); its purpose seems to be to drive away intruders." On the 2nd April and subsequent days, this bird attacked every other male that approached, and not only maintained its position but ultimately succeeded in securing a mate. Here then we have two territories occupied by two males, both of which had obtained a mate. The relation of these two birds was normal, a month's routine had defined their boundaries, and conflicts were less frequent than formerly. But upon this comparatively peaceful scene a strange male intrudes. Observe the manner of the intrusion. The stranger does not wander about first in this direction and then in that, but acts *as if* it had some definite end in view, and establishing itself in a small alder bush which it uses as a base or headquarters, it gradually extends its dominion, gains the mastery over the surrounding ground, part of which belonged to No. 1 male and part to No. 2, and finally drives a wedge, so to speak, between the two territories.

How is its behaviour to be explained, and why did its presence cause such commotion? No one could have watched the gradual unfolding of this incident day by day and not have been impressed by the persistent endeavour with which this male maintained its position in one small part of the meadow. This is the first and most important consideration. Then there is 106 the attitude, also significant, which it adopted towards the females; for I take it that, apart from the question of territory, the explanation of its intrusion must be sought in the necessity for securing a mate—that it was attracted by the presence of the females, and that the proximate end of its behaviour was the possession of one of them. But if there is one thing that emerges from the facts more clearly than another it is that the course of its behaviour was in no way influenced by the presence or absence of either of the females. My reasons for saying so are the following: in the first place, it made no attempt to pursue or to thrust its attention upon either one or the other of them; secondly, it even went so far as to attack and drive them away when they approached too closely; and in the third place, when an unpaired female did at length appear, it adopted a different attitude and forthwith paired. And bearing in mind that these two females had already been with their respective mates for some considerable time, and that there was reason to believe that coition had actually taken place, is it likely that any counter-attraction would have proved successful in tempting either of them away from its mate, or probable, if they were the sole attraction, that the intruding male would have been so persistent in remaining? How very much simpler it is to fit the pieces together, if for the time being we ignore the female and fix our attention upon the territory. Each item of behaviour then falls into its proper place, and the fighting which 107 seemed so perplexing and meaningless becomes a factor of prime importance. First of all the male arrives; then it establishes itself in a small alder bush and advertises its presence by song; next, by persistent effort in attacking the neighbouring males, it frees a piece of ground from their dominion; and finally, in proper sequence, a female arrives, pairing takes place, and reproduction is secured.

A battle between two pairs of Jays

How then does the whole matter stand? If it were males only that engaged in serious conflict, and if they fought only in the presence of a female, the problem would resolve itself into one simply of obtaining mates. But the warfare extends in a variety of directions, it is not confined to one sex, nor to unpaired individuals, nor need the opponents necessarily be of the same sex; it involves both sexes alike singly or combined. Now the view that the biological end of battle is, in its primary aspect, related to the female, cannot, as we have seen, apply to the conflicts between different pairs, and only by much stretching of the imagination can it be held responsible for the hostility that males frequently display towards females or *vice versa*. It is valid only for a certain form of warfare. But that form represents, you will say, a large proportion of the whole, which is true; and so long as we ignore the remainder, we might rest content in the belief that we had solved the major part of the problem. But can we ignore the remainder? Can we say that the conflicts between paired males, for example, are 108 simply offshoots of the pugnacious disposition, and have no part to play in the process of reproduction? They recur with marked persistency season after season and generation after generation; they are to be found in species widely remote; they are frequent in occurrence; and no one who had observed them and noted the vigour with which they are conducted, could, I think, conclude that they were meaningless—and be satisfied. They must somehow be explained. So that if anyone thinks fit to maintain that possession of a mate is an adequate explanation of part of the hostilities, it is clearly impossible to regard all the fighting as a manifestation of one principle directed towards a common biological end.

But wherever we extend our researches, we find that the facts give precision to the view that the occupation of a territory is the condition under which the pugnacious instinct is rendered susceptible to stimulation. The Lapwing, when in its territory, displays hostility towards other males of its own species, but when upon neutral ground, treats them with indifference; the Chiffchaff pursues its rival up to the boundary and is then apparently satisfied that its object has been achieved; the cock Chaffinch in March permits no other male to intrude upon its acre or so of ground during the early hours of the morning, but for the rest of the day it joins the flock and is sociable; the Herring-Gull resents the approach of strangers so long as it occupies its few square feet of cliff, but welcomes companions 109 whilst it is following the plough—all of which points to a relation between the territory and the fighting. And this view has at least one merit—it accounts for all the fighting no matter what degree of severity may be reached or in what way the sexes may be involved. The complexity of the strife presents no obstacle; for if the biological end of the fighting is to render the territory, which has already been established, secure from intrusion, each sex will have its allotted part to play at the allotted time: thus the battles between the males before females appear on the scene will decide the initial question of ownership; those between the females will give an advantage to the more virile members and insure an even distribution of mates for the successful males; the constant struggles between paired males will roughly maintain the boundaries and prevent such encroachment as might hamper the supply of food for the young; and the co-operation of male and female in defence of the territory will be an additional safeguard. Each form of battle will contribute some share towards the main biological function of reproduction.

Hitherto we have dealt principally with the male. We have referred, it is true, to the fact that the female co-operates with her mate in order to drive away intruders, but beyond this, we have made no attempt to trace what part, if any, she plays in the whole scheme. We must do so now. 110

The various steps by which the territory is not only established but made secure from invasion, imply an inherited nature nicely balanced in many directions—first of all the male must be so attuned as to be ready to search for a territory at the right moment; then it must be capable of selecting a suitable environment; and, having established itself, it must be prepared to defend its area from a rival, and to resist encroachment by its neighbours—and if it failed in any one of these respects, it would run the risk of failure in the attainment of reproduction. Each individual has therefore to pass, so to speak, through a number of sieves—the meshes of which are none too wide—before it can have a reasonable prospect of success. This being so, we ask, in the first place, whether the female, too, may not have an eliminating test to pass; and in the second place, whether she may not also assist in furthering the biological end of securing the territory.

Now the answer to the first of these questions will be found to be in the affirmative. Just as, in the securing of a territory, the ultimate appeal is to the physical strength of the male, so, in the course of her search for a mate, the female may be called upon to challenge, or may be challenged by a rival, and the issue is decided by force. My attention was first drawn to this fact by a struggle between two female Whitethroats, which I have described elsewhere. The scene of its occurrence was the corner of a small osier bed occupied by one male, and the females 111 that took part in it had only recently arrived, but the male, an unpaired bird, had been in possession of its territory for some days. The sequel to this struggle, which was protracted and severe, was the disappearance of both females, the male being left without a mate for a further ten days.

The female Chaffinch shares in the defence of the territory and attacks other females.

Numerous instances have since come under my notice. Hen Chaffinches become so absorbed that they fall to the ground and there continue the struggle. Seizing hold of one another by the feathers of the head, they roll from side to side, and then, without relaxing their grip, lie exhausted—the quickened heart-beat, altered respiration, tightly compressed feathers and partially expanded wings betraying the intensity of the conflict.

As the breeding season approaches, hen Blackbirds grow more pugnacious. Individuals that early in the year have frequented the same spot daily and have ever shown every sign of friendship, become openly hostile. For two years in succession I had an opportunity of observing females under such conditions, and of studying the gradual change in their relationship. Each morning at break of day and for some hours afterwards they could be seen in the same place, one following the other as they searched for food first in this direction and then in that, as if they derived some special pleasure from the fact of their companionship. Then a change began to manifest itself. Indications of animosity became apparent; one would run 112 towards the other in a threatening attitude and, in a half-hearted manner, peck at it; and gradually the hostility grew, until the tentative pecking developed into a scuffle and the scuffle into a conflict.

Much fighting also occurs between the females of the Reed-Bunting, and likewise between those of the Moor-Hen, and because these two species are not only common but inhabit respectively open stretches of marshy ground or large sheets of water, the fighting can be readily observed.

Why do the females fight before they are definitely paired? To obtain mates? This certainly seems to be the obvious explanation because any question of securing territory can be excluded; yet if it be true that their sex is numerically inferior, it is difficult to understand the necessity for such strenuous competition. But what is the condition under which the pugnacious instinct of the female is rendered susceptible to stimulation? It cannot be merely the presence of a male ready to breed, for then there would be endless commotion amongst the flocks of Chaffinches or of Lapwings which in March are composed of both sexes, including even males that have secured territories. There must be some other circumstance; and, judging by experience, it is to be found in the territory—a male, that is to say, in occupation of one, is the condition under which the inherited nature of the female is allowed free play. We must bear in mind, however, that the competition 113 between the males is very severe, that large numbers probably fail to pass even this preliminary test, and that only a proportion are in a position to offer to the female the condition under which her process can successfully run its course; so that the presumption is—though it is incapable of demonstration—that there is a competition for such males each recurring season, and that, on the average, the weaker females fail to procreate their kind.

But apart from any direct assistance she may give in driving away intruders, does she in any way help to further the biological end of reproduction? This is a difficult question to answer, and the suggestion I have to make can only apply in those cases in which the territory is occupied throughout the breeding season. Much of the fighting between the males occurs in her presence, and it must be admitted—though it is difficult to speak with any degree of certainty—that such fighting, taken as a whole, bears the stamp of exceptional determination. Let us then grant that the excitement of a male does, under these circumstances, reach a higher level of intensity, and let us see how this will add to the security of the territory. The fact that the male has established itself and obtained a mate is not alone sufficient to accomplish the end for which the territory has been evolved. During the period between the initial discharge of the sexual function and the time when incubation draws to a close, much may happen to prejudice the future of the offspring; there 114 is always the possibility of invasion by an individual whose development is backward or which has been unsuccessful in making good the first step, and, as we saw in the case of the Reed-Bunting, a portion of the ground won may be lost; there is always the danger of gradual encroachment by neighbouring owners; and there is even a possibility that a pair may be so persistently harassed by more virile neighbours as to forsake the locality permanently. If then a male is to attain a full measure of success it must be capable of keeping its boundaries intact up to the time when the young are able to fend for themselves, and consequently it is important that its intolerant nature should remain susceptible to stimulation throughout the greater part of the season.

Does the presence of a female serve to promote this end? Now we know very little of the influence exerted by one sex upon the other. Professor Lloyd Morgan has suggested that the male raises the emotional tone of the female, a suggestion which seems to me in accordance with the facts. There is reason to believe, however, that the converse is also true—namely that the excitement of the male reaches a higher level of intensity when a female is present. Granting then that his emotional tone is raised, how will this affect the question? So great is the difference of opinion as to the part that the emotions play in furthering the life of the individual that one hesitates to accept any particular one. But it seems to be generally 115 admitted that emotion adds to the efficacy of behaviour, and this is the view of Professor Lloyd Morgan. "Whatever may be the exact psychological nature of the emotions, it may be regarded," he says, "as certain that they introduce into the conscious situation elements which contribute not a little to the energy of behaviour. They are important conditions to vigorous and sustained conation." Therefore, if it be true that the female raises the emotional tone of the male, the result will be an increased flow of energy into all the specific modes of behaviour connected with reproduction, amongst which those directly concerned in the securing and defence of the territory will receive their share; so that instead of a progressive weakening of just those elements in the situation which make for success, the level of their efficiency will be maintained as a result of such reinforcement. But the female becomes intolerant of her own sex when she has discovered a male ready to breed, and, later, assists her mate in resisting intrusion; and by raising her emotional tone, he may be the means of furthering more strenuous behaviour on her part. Each member of the pair would in this way contribute towards the energy of behaviour of its mate, and hence add indirectly to the security of the territory.

It may be well to illustrate the foregoing remarks. Suppose that there is a small piece of woodland barely sufficient to hold three pairs of Willow-Warblers, and suppose that the male and female in the middle territory did not respond to 116 one another's influence quite as readily as the adjoining males and females, what would be the result? The emotional tone of the central pair would stand at a lower level of intensity; and, since their congenital dispositions would lack the necessary reinforcement, the birds would tend to become less and less punctilious in keeping their boundaries intact, whereas the adjoining pairs, always on the alert and meeting with little opposition, would encroach more and more and gradually extend their dominion. And so, by the time the young were hatched, the parents would be in occupation of an area too limited in extent to insure the necessarily rapid supply of food, and would be compelled to intrude upon the adjoining ground. But knowing how routine becomes ingrained in the life of the individual, knowing that for weeks this pair had submitted to their neighbours, can we believe that they would be capable of asserting their authority and that the young would be properly cared for? Or suppose that different pairs of Kittiwake Gulls on the crowded ledges, or different pairs of Puffins in the crowded burrows, varied in like manner, would they all have equal chances of rearing their offspring? The struggle for reproduction is nowhere more severe than amongst the cliff-breeding sea birds; it is not for nothing that one sees Kittiwake Gulls, locked together, fall into the water hundreds of feet below and struggle to the point of exhaustion, or, as has been reported, to the point of death; it is not for nothing that Puffins fight 117 with such desperation. And surely success will be attained by that pair whose emotional tone stands high and whose impulse to fight is therefore strong, rather than to the ill-assorted couple.

The argument, then, is briefly this. In the spring, a marked change takes place in the character of the males of very many species; instead of being gregarious they either avoid one another and become hostile, or, if their conditions of existence require that they shall still live together, they become irritable and pugnacious. This change is made known to us by the battles of varying degrees of severity which are such a feature of bird life in the spring; and since a female can commonly be observed to accompany the combatants, the possession of a mate appears at first sight to be the proximate end for which the males are contending. But when the circumstances which lead up to the quarrels are investigated closely, the problem becomes more difficult; for it is not merely a question of males fighting in the presence of a female, as is generally supposed to be the case, but on the contrary there is a complexity of strife which is bewildering—males attack females or *vice versa*; female fights with female; or a pair combine to drive away another pair, or even a solitary individual no matter of which sex. This complexity of strife makes against the view that the possession of a mate is the reason of the fighting. But an even stronger objection is to be found in the fact 118 that males are hostile when no female is present—and hence we must seek elsewhere for the true explanation.

Now if the behaviour of a male be closely observed, it will be found that its pugnacious instinct gains or loses susceptibility according to the position which it happens to occupy—when its ground is trespassed upon, the impulse to fight is strong; but when it crosses the boundary it seems to lose all interest in the intruder. Moreover, in some species, the male rejoins the flock at intervals during the early part of the season and for a time leads a double existence, passing backwards and forwards between its territory and the neutral ground. Its behaviour under these circumstances affords some valuable evidence, for the bird displays little if any hostility when accompanying the flock, yet when it returns to the ground over which it exercises dominion, no male can approach without being attacked. The conclusion, therefore, seems to be inevitable, namely that the actual occupation of a territory is the condition under which the pugnacious nature of the male is rendered susceptible to appropriate stimulation.
119

CHAPTER IV
THE RELATION OF SONG TO THE TERRITORY

If we listen to the voices of the Waders as, in search of food, they follow the slowly ebbing tide, we shall notice that each species has a number of different cries, some of which are uttered frequently and others only occasionally. Not only so, but if we study the circumstances under which they are uttered, we shall in time learn to associate certain specific notes with certain definite situations.

The Curlew, when surprised, utters a cry with which most of us, I suppose, are familiar; but when with lowered head it drives away another individual from the feeding ground, it gives expression to its feelings by a low, raucous sound, which again is different from its cry when a Common Gull steals the *arenicola* that has been drawn out of the mud with such labour.

Thus we come to speak of "alarm notes," "notes of anger," "warning notes"—naming each according to the situations which normally accompany their utterance. And so, all species, 120 or at least a large majority of them, have, in greater or lesser variety, cries and calls which are peculiar to certain seasons and certain situations; and since on many occasions we have indisputable evidence of the utility of the sound produced—as when, upon the alarm being given by one individual, the flock of Lapwing rises, or when, in response to a particular note of the parent, the nestling Blackcap ceases to call—so are we bound to infer that all the cries are, in one way or another, serviceable in furthering the life of the individual.

But besides these call-notes, birds produce special sounds during the season of reproduction—some by instrument, others by voice, others again by the aid of mechanical device. And not only is this the case, but many accompany their songs with peculiar flights, such as soaring to a great height, or circling, or floating in the air upon outstretched wings. These special sounds and special flights are those with which I now propose to deal, including under the heading "song" all sounds whether harsh or monotonous or beautiful, and whether vocally or otherwise produced; and I shall endeavour to show not only that they are related to the "territory," but that they contribute not a little to the successful attainment of reproduction.

The vocal productions are infinite in variety and combination. At the one extreme we have songs composed of a single note repeated 121 slowly or rapidly as the case may be, whilst at the other we have the complex productions of the Warblers; and between these two extremes, notes and phrases are combined and recombined in ways innumerable. And just as there is a rich variety of combination, so there is a very wide variation in the purity and character of the notes—some are harsh, others melodious, some flute-like, others more of a whistle, and others again such as can only be likened to the notes of a stringed instrument. Hence in variety of phrase combination added to variety in the character of the note, there is a possibility of infinite modes of expression.

If, in the latter part of May, we take up a position at dawn in some osier bed, we listen to songs which have reached a high degree of specialisation, songs, moreover, which appeal to us on account of their beauty; if, on the other hand, we climb down the face of the sea cliff, we hear an entirely different class of songs—harsh, guttural, weird, monotonous sounds, which, appeal to us though they may, lack the music of the voices in the osier bed. And just as, in the osier bed, we can recognise each species by its voice, so we can distinguish the "cackle" of the Fulmar, the "croak" of the Guillemot, or the "grunt" of the Shag. In the osier bed, however, there is considerable variation in the song of different individuals of the same species, so much so that we can recognise this one from that; whereas on the cliff we cannot distinguish between the voices of different individuals. And the more highly developed the song, the greater the range of variation appears to be; but notwithstanding this—notwithstanding the fact that the pitch may differ, the phrase combination may differ, and the timbre may differ—the song remains nevertheless specific. So that the two principal features of "song," broadly speaking, are "diversity" and "specific character."

In contrast with the call-notes, the majority of which can be heard at all times of the year, the song is restricted as a rule to one season, and that one the season of reproduction. It is true, of course, that some birds sing during the autumn, and, if the climatic conditions are favourable, in the winter also, just as others betray, in the autumn, symptoms of emotional manifestation peculiar to the spring; but just as the manifestation of the latter is feeble and vestigial, so, too, does the song of the former lack the vigour and persistency which is characteristic of the spring. Again, in contrast with the call-notes, which are common alike to both sexes, song is confined to one sex—a peculiar property of the males.

Now all, I think, will agree that it must serve some biological purpose—this at least seems to be the conclusion to be drawn from the two outstanding features of "diversity" and "specific character"; and since the voices of different individuals of the same species vary, it has been suggested that, by creating a more effective pairing situation, it is serviceable in furthering the life of the individual. I do not propose at the moment to enquire whether this doctrine be true, but rather to direct attention to other ways in which the song may be useful.

Is the instinct susceptible to stimulation under all conditions during the season of reproduction, or only under some well-defined condition? This is the question to which we will first direct inquiry.

Song in its full development belongs, as we have seen, to the season of reproduction; it is heard at the dawn of the seasonal sexual process, and is the most conspicuous outward manifestation of the internal organic changes which ultimately lead to reproduction. These changes would appear, at first sight, to be the primary condition which renders the instinct susceptible to appropriate stimulation. But while this is true up to a point, in so far, that is to say, as organic changes are a necessary antecedent of all behaviour connected with the attainment of reproduction, closer acquaintance with the circumstances under which the instinct is allowed full play leads to the belief that they are not alone sufficient to account for the facts as observed. In order to arrive at a decision we must seek out the specific factors in the external environment with which "song" is definitely related.

Some birds cross whole continents on their way to the breeding grounds, others travel many miles, others again find suitable accommodation in a neighbouring parish—nearly all have a journey to perform, it may be short or it may be long. The flocks of Finches gradually decrease and we observe the males scattering in different directions in search of territories; we watch the summer migrants on their way—small parties halting for a few hours in the hedgerows and then continuing their journey, single individuals alighting on trees and bushes and resting there for a few minutes, and the constant passage of flocks of various dimensions at various altitudes; and we see Fieldfares, Redwings, and Bramblings slowly making their way from the south and the west to their homes in the far north. Occasionally we hear their song, not the emotional outburst customary at this season, but, except in isolated cases, a weak and tentative performance. Gätke speaks of the absence of song on the Island of Heligoland, and refers to the Whitethroat as one of the few migrants that enliven that desolate rock with their melody. On the other hand, many migrants that rest temporarily on the Isle of May sing vigorously. 5 But on the whole there is, I think, no question that the male whilst travelling to its breeding grounds, and, even after its arrival, whilst in search of a territory, sings but little—and that little lacks the persistency characteristic of the period of sexual activity. Yet, when a suitable territory is eventually secured, the nature of the bird seems to change; for, instead of being silent and retiring, as if aware of some end not fully attained, it not only makes itself conspicuous but advertises its presence by a song uttered with such perseverance as to suggest that that end is at length attained. Hence, in a general way, the instinct of song seems to be related to the establishment of a territory.

Now the subsequent course of behaviour tends to confirm this view. We have already had occasion to refer to the fact that the males of some species desert their territories temporarily and join together on ground which is regarded by the birds that associate there as neutral, and that they do so not merely for the purpose of securing food but because they derive some special pleasure from the act of association, and we shall find that the altered behaviour of the male when it leaves its territory to seek food or to join the flock is an important point for us just now.

Buntings desert their territories temporarily and collect in flocks on the newly sown fields of grain. Some of the males are single, others are paired, and accompanied, it may be, by their mates; they wander over the ground in search of food, uttering their call-notes from time to time, or, settling upon the hedges and trees surrounding the field, rest there and preen their feathers. But even though a male may be surrounded by other males, even though it may occupy a position where it is conspicuous to all around, even though, that is to say, it is apparently in contact with just those stimulating circumstances which will evoke a response when it returns to its territory, yet it makes no attempt to sing.

Lapwings, when they resort to the

neutral ground, run this way and that in full enjoyment of one another's companionship, behaving as they do when they flock in autumn and winter. Specific emotional manifestation is, however, absent, and their actions seem to be in nowise affected by the powerful impulse which only a few minutes previously determined their conduct, for of the characteristic flight with its accompanying cry there is no sign.

Early in the season Turtle Doves often collect from the surrounding country at certain spots where their favourite food is abundant. The croak of this Dove—its true song—is a familiar sound during the summer, but in addition the bird has a sexual note characteristic of the race. I watched a flock of upwards of one hundred on some derelict ground approximately eight acres in extent. Here, in May, the birds were attracted by the seeds of *Stellaria media* which was growing in profusion. After 5 A.M. there was continuous traffic between this piece of ground and the surrounding neighbourhood, a constant arrival and departure of single individuals or pairs; and, as they fed, the sexual note could be heard in all directions. Now some of the males occupied territories close at hand, and one could watch their passage to and fro; 127 yet in no single instance did I hear the true song uttered on the feeding ground, although the moment a male returned to its territory its monotonous croak could be heard, uttered moreover with that persistence which is so marked a feature of all song or of the sounds that correspond to it.

Thus it will be seen that, even after the internal organic changes have taken place, the instinct of song is not susceptible to stimulation at all times and under all circumstances, but only at certain specified times and under special circumstances which can be observed to correspond with the occupation of the territory.

In many species each male singles out within its territory some prominent position to which it resorts with growing frequency. This position is an important feature of the territory, and exercises a dominating influence on the life of the bird. I have referred to it as the "headquarters," and it may be a solitary tree or bush, an outstanding mound or mole hillock, a gatepost or a railing—anything in fact that supplies a convenient resting place so long as it fulfils one condition, namely that the bird when it is there is conspicuous. It need not, however, be a tree or a mound or indeed anything upon which the bird can perch, for there is reason to think that the soaring flight undertaken at this season by so many males, since it is generally accompanied by the specific sexual sound, 128 answers the same purpose as the topmost branch of a tree.

Now there is nothing in the external environment to which the song is more definitely related than to the "headquarters"—this at least is the conclusion to be drawn from the behaviour, and I will indicate the sort of evidence upon which such conclusion is based. There is, first of all, the persistency with which the male resorts to the same tree, even to the same branch, and, as it seems, solely for the purpose of advertisement. We know by experience the approximate routine of the male's behaviour; we know where to seek it, where to hear it, and when once we have discovered its headquarters, we know that there it will sing day after day for weeks or it may be for months together—perhaps the most striking feature of its behaviour at this season. Next, we find that other trees, though made use of, are not made use of to a similar extent for the purpose of song. The area occupied varies much according to the nature of the environment; it is sometimes extensive, and seldom less than half an acre or so in extent; but in most instances it contains plenty of trees and bushes which could, one would imagine, serve the purpose of a "headquarters" just as well as the particular one selected, and yet the bird, when there, betrays no inclination to sing at all comparable with that which can be observed when it occupies its accustomed perch. Further evidence is afforded in the behaviour of those 129 species that make temporary excursions from their territories. The male, on its return, flies as a rule direct to its special tree and sings. Sometimes, however, it settles upon the ground, not unfrequently accompanied by the female, and while there remains silent; but presently rising from the ground and deserting its mate, it flies to the headquarters and sings. Again, nearly every male at one time or another in the course of the season is aroused to action by the intrusion of a rival. The emotional tone of the owner of the territory is then raised, and the intruder is pursued and attacked; but this alone is not sufficient, it seems as if the chain of instinctive activities, when once aroused by appropriate stimulation, must pursue its course to the end—and the end in such a case is only reached and complete satisfaction only gained when the bird has not merely returned to his "headquarters" but has given vocal expression to his emotion. Finally, we must bear in mind these two facts, that the "headquarters" is occupied solely by the male—it forms no part of the life of the female—and that it is the male only that sings.

Many such subtle incidents of behaviour as the foregoing can be perceived but not readily described, and trifling though they may seem to be in themselves, yet in the aggregate they yield full assurance of a close relationship.

The distant song of a male, or the presence of an intruding male, have also stimulating effects, though in somewhat different ways. 130 The former evokes the normal reply, that is to say the bird, if silent, is liable to utter a corresponding reply; the latter arouses hostility into which is infused much feeling tone, the bird sings hurriedly while in pursuit of its rival, and, which is more remarkable still, even in the midst of an encounter. Both the normal reply and the emotional song must be similar in origin—different aspects of the same situation—and both are clearly related to the other male.

The arrival of a female may also be followed by an emotional outburst which can be heard at intervals for some days; on the other hand, the song may continue as before or, for a time, entirely cease.

To take the emotional outburst first. This would appear to be susceptible of explanation on the hypothesis that the voice contributes to a more effective pairing situation; an hypothesis which admittedly, at first sight, gains some support from the fact that a second or a third male is frequently present. But, in truth, the presence of a second male makes the situation, so far as the relationship between the song and the female is concerned, all the more perplexing; for, as we have already seen, the instinct of pugnacity, when aroused by the appearance of an intruder, is also liable to be accompanied by a similarly extravagant song. On each occasion the vocal effort is infused with much feeling tone, and it would be impossible to point to any one feature which is peculiar to only one 131 occasion. The question therefore arises as to whether the emotional outburst which we are attributing to the arrival of a female may not after all be due to the presence of an intruding male. It may be so. But although I can recall no single instance in which the presence of an intruder could be definitely excluded, yet I should hesitate to base upon this any broad generalisation.

When the normal course of the song is not interrupted by the arrival of a female, when, that is to say, the male still pursues the routine to which he has all along been accustomed, and still sings at stated intervals in stated places with a voice that betrays no heightened emotional tone, even though the song may convey some meaning to the delicate perceptual powers of the female, we have nothing to lay hold upon which can be construed as an indication of direct relationship between the song and the presence of the female.

The partial or complete suspension of the song after pairing has taken place is the most interesting, as it is the most noticeable, feature. Not that it is by any means universal—if it were so, some of the difficulties that beset the path of interpretation would be removed, but it is sufficiently widespread to demand explanation. In nearly every case it is, however, only temporary, the period during which the male is silent varying from a few days to a few weeks. The male Grasshopper-Warbler, when it first reaches us, sings persistently, but 132 when it is joined by a female a change becomes apparent; instead of the incessant trill, there are spasmodic outbursts of short duration, and in the course of a few days the bird lapses into a silence which may be broken for a short while at dawn, or late in the evening, but is often complete. More striking still is the change in the case of the Marsh-Warbler, and the sudden deterioration, or even suspension, of strains so beautiful and so varied, at a moment, too, when it might least be expected, at once arrests the attention. The Reed-Warbler that had its headquarters in a willow sang vigorously from the middle of May until a female arrived on the 20th June, when its voice was hushed, except for occasional outbursts which lacked force and were of short duration. When the Wood-Warbler secures a territory it repeats its sibilant trill with unwearying zeal, yet no sooner does a mate appear than its emotion is manifested in other directions. The Reed-Bunting is vociferous during February and March; but when a female arrives, periods of silence are frequent and the instinct of the bird becomes progressively less susceptible to stimulation. After the manner of the race the male makes temporary excursions from its territory accompanied by his mate, and it is noteworthy that when he returns and she is absent he sings, but that the moment she joins him, or even comes into sight, he is silent. In fact, in greater or less degree, a change is noticeable in the song of many resident and migratory species 133 under similar circumstances, a deterioration so marked that we learn by experience to regard it as a certain indication of the arrival of a mate.

Thus it becomes clear that there are certain specific factors in the external environment with which the instinct can be definitely related, and in the order of their importance they are (1) the territory as a whole; (2) the headquarters; (3) an intruding male; (4) the female.

To what extent are these relationships interrelated? Are they all mutually dependent upon one another, or is there one which conditions the remainder?

In the first place it is evident that if a male were not to establish a territory, no opportunity would be afforded for making use of any special post or for acquiring a habit in relation to it, and so without further consideration we may say that the connection between the song and the headquarters, whatever it may be, is primarily dependent upon the establishment of a territory.

Next, we have the fact that the distant voice, or still more so the presence, of another male has an exciting influence and evokes a corresponding reply. Here we have a direct relationship, and one which at first sight appears to be exclusive of cross-correlation. But is it really so; does no circumstance arise under which even the proximity of a rival fails to evoke response? The reply is not doubtful. Such a circumstance *does* arise—when a male for one reason or another 134 passes outside the limits of its accustomed area. This aspect of behaviour has already been fully discussed in connection with the question of hostility, and everyone, I imagine, must by now be pretty well familiar with the facts. However, it does not often happen that we are given such an aid to interpretation as is vouchsafed to us in the altered behaviour of the male when it joins the flock, and if, as I believe, song and hostility are intimately associated, forming part of an inter-related whole which, for biological interpretation, has, as its end, the attainment of reproduction, it is not surprising that circumstances which lead to the modification of the one should likewise affect the other; I offer no apology, therefore, for adverting to this aspect of behaviour once again.

Now a male may leave its territory for three reasons—to pursue an intruder, to join the flock on neutral ground, or to find the necessary means of subsistence on other feeding grounds. On each of these occasions it hears the song of, and is in close contact with, other males; and if the relationship of which we are speaking be really exclusive of cross-correlation, its instinct ought to respond with the customary freedom. But what happens? A male pursues its rival, betraying much emotion and singing extravagantly, until the boundary is passed, when emotion subsides and it is silent; or, it flies to the flock on neutral ground, and, although surrounded by the very males that a short time 135 previously evoked response, is there unresponsive; or again, it goes in search of food and collects with other males bent on a similar errand, and in presence of what we know would be an exciting influence under other circumstances, it nevertheless remains silent. Hence the relationship between the song and a male rival seems, as in the case of the headquarters, to depend in the first instance upon the occupation of a territory.

So that the relationship between the song and the territory as a whole is clearly of a different order from that which obtains between the song and the headquarters, or the song and a male rival; for the first, as far as can be judged by observation, is exclusive of, whilst the second and the third involve, cross-correlation. How are these facts to be explained? We have already seen that it belongs to the nature of the male during the season of reproduction to establish itself in a definite place, and this action is just as much a part of its hereditary nature as the building of the nest is of that of the female, and it is just as necessary for the successful attainment of reproduction. What exactly the stimulus is to this mode of behaviour we do not know; we can go no further back than the internal organic changes which are known to occur and which we assume, not without some reason, are responsible for its initiation. Granting, then, that there is this congenital disposition, what relation does it bear to the song? Without a doubt the song is likewise 136 founded upon a congenital basis; it is truly instinctive, and as such requires appropriate stimulation; furthermore the male sings only when in occupation of its territory. Having regard to these two facts we might say that the territory is the stimulus to the song. But this can scarcely be a true interpretation, for inasmuch as the stimulus would be relatively constant, a relatively constant response ought to follow, and even a slight acquaintance with the daily round of behaviour will furnish plenty of evidence to the contrary, seeing that the song, though persistent, is never continuous—in fact there are long periods of silence during the daytime, and only in the morning and the evening does the male become really vociferous. What then is the stimulus? Through awareness of something in the environment the male responds to stimulation, and the only reply we can give is that the headquarters, or a distant song, or the proximity of another male—with all of which, as we have seen, the instinct is definitely related—are the specific factors which normally evoke response—and experience teaches us that the periods of quiescence are just those when life is at its lowest ebb and these stimulating factors less in evidence. Bearing this in mind, bearing in mind the fact that when a male joins the flock or crosses the boundary its instinct ceases to respond, bearing, that is to say, that there is evidence of relationship between these specific factors and the song only when the territory is actually occu 137 pied, the conclusion seems inevitable that we have here the determining condition which renders the instinct susceptible to appropriate stimulation.

There remains the female. I place her last in order of importance, not because I regard her influence as of small consequence, but because the evidence is of a varied and complex kind, so much so that it is difficult to ascertain by observation just how far she is a situational item. It will be remembered that the only direct evidence we had of such influence was a deterioration or, in some instances, a complete cessation of vocal manifestation Clearly then we are confronted with a relationship of a different kind from that which we have been discussing; for not only is anything in the nature of stimulation absent, but, and this is a remarkable fact, the other items in the environment which formerly evoked response no longer do so in quite the same way. Is there any awareness on the part of the male of the relation between his voice and the mate that is to be, or is it merely that as the sexual situation increases in complexity some inhibiting influence comes into play? These are questions which lead up to difficult problems. But it is no part of my task to discuss the psychological aspect of the behaviour; my purpose is merely to show that the situation on the arrival of a female undergoes marked modification, that the instinct of the male is then less susceptible to stimulation, and that the factors in the external environment 138 which formerly elicited response become relatively neutral.

Hence the appearance of the female on the scene marks the opening of a new stage in the life-history of the male, and, to judge by the course of events, it would seem as if the song with its network of relationships had now served its main biological purpose.

And now, what is the purpose, and what the origin, of song? Is it, as some naturalists have conceived, a means of raising the emotional tone of the female, of creating a more effective pairing situation, and so of removing a barrier to the successful discharge of the sexual function; or, is the emphasis here too much upon the emotional, too little upon the strictly utilitarian, aspect? All, I think, will agree that it must serve some biological purpose, and the position we have so far reached is that the determining condition of its manifestation is not merely the establishment, but the actual occupation of a territory, and that there are no factors in the external environment which can evoke response in the absence of such condition. This being so, the further questions arise as to whether it contributes towards the attainment of the end for which the whole territorial system has been built up, and what precisely is the way in which it does so.

Everyone knows that in the spring the shyest of birds no longer practise the art of concealment. The Curlew soars to a great height, and upon outstretched wings hovers in 139 the air whilst uttering its plaintive wail; the cock Grouse, as if dissatisfied with its "crowing," springs into the air and becomes a conspicuous object of the moor; the wary Redshank, poised on flickering wings, forgets its mournful alarm cry, and finds again its melodious song; and even the secretive Grasshopper-Warbler crawls out of the midst of the thicket in order to "reel," just as, for a similar reason, Savi's Warbler climbs to the top of a tall reed. In fact the males of most species, when they are finally established on the breeding grounds, make themselves as conspicuous as possible by sight and by sound. And since the sounds produced by no two species are exactly alike, the females are able to recognise their prospective mates, and the males that are still in search of ground have ample warning if that upon which they are treading is already occupied. So that you see, from the remarkable development of the vocal powers in the male, there follow two important results—"recognition" and "warning."

We here turn from song as the expression of an instinctive disposition, and the question of what calls forth this expression, to the impression produced by the song on the hearer.

Most birds have a call-note or a number of call-notes, which, generally speaking, are specifically distinct. But to the human ear they are not always so, perhaps because our power of hearing is less sensitive than that of a bird, and unable to appreciate delicate differences of tone. Be this as it may, however, the fact remains that we 140 often find it difficult, and in not a few cases impossible, to recognise a bird merely by its call. The plaintive notes of the Willow-Warbler and of the Chiffchaff are to our ears very closely akin, so, too, are those of the Marsh-Warbler and of the Reed-Warbler, and there is a great resemblance between the hissing sound produced by the two Whitethroats. In Co. Donegal I have been deceived by the spring-call of the Chaffinch which, owing possibly to the humidity of the atmosphere, is, there, almost indistinguishable from the corresponding note of the Greenfinch. The Yellow Bunting and the Cirl Bunting frequently make use of a similar note, so do the Curlew and the Whimbrel. In fact, numberless instances could be quoted in which notes appear to us identical, and, as a rule, the more closely related the species, the more difficult it becomes to distinguish the sounds—alike in plumage, alike in behaviour, alike in emotional manifestation, it would be surprising if they were not alike in voice. But the moment we pass from the call-notes to a consideration of the songs we are faced with a very remarkable fact, for not only are these readily distinguished, but in many cases they bear no resemblance in any single characteristic. What could be more unlike than the songs of the Willow-Warbler and of the Chiffchaff, of the Marsh-Warbler and the Reed-Warbler, or of the Yellow Bunting and the Cirl Bunting?

Now when different individuals collect in flocks at certain seasons, they assist one another 141 in finding food, and afford mutual protection by giving timely warning of the approach of a common enemy, and the gregarious instinct is thus of great advantage to the species; but no matter how powerful the impulse to flock might be, if there were no adequate means of communication, the different units would frequently fail to discover their neighbours. Here the specific cries and calls come into play, enabling them as they move about in search of food, or change their feeding grounds, or whilst they are on migration, to keep constantly in touch with one another; and hence one purpose that these call-notes serve is that of recognition. Moreover, they convey their meaning to individuals of other species and are acted upon, and are thus in every sense socially serviceable; but on the other hand, whilst there is much evidence to show that the song is of great individual value, there is none to show that it is in any like manner of direct advantage to the community.

If, then, there is in the call-notes an adequate means of communication and of recognition, why do I suggest that the song has also been evolved primarily for the purpose of recognition?

What, first of all, are the conditions in the life behaviour during the season of reproduction that make the intervention of the voice a consideration of such importance? The general result of our investigation might be summed up thus: we found that the male inherits a disposition to secure a territory, that at the proper season this disposition comes into functional 142 activity and leads to its establishment in a definite place, and that it cannot search for a mate because its freedom of action in this respect is forbidden by law; that the female inherits no such disposition, that she is free to move from place to place, free to satisfy her predominant inclination, and to seek a mate where she wills; and, since the appropriate organic condition which leads to pairing must coincide with appropriate conditions in the environment, that the union of the sexes must be accomplished without undue delay. Furthermore we found that a territory is essential if the offspring are to be successfully reared; that, since the available breeding ground is limited, competition for it is severe, and that the male is precluded from leaving the ground which he has selected, and is obliged, in order to secure a mate, to make himself conspicuous. That was our general result. Now there are two ways by which the male can make himself conspicuous—by occupying such a position that he can be readily seen, or by producing some special sound which will be audible to the female and direct her to the spot. The former, by itself, is insufficient; in the dim light of the early dawn, when life is at its highest, and mating proceeds apace, what aid would it be for a male to perch on the topmost branch of a tree, how slender a guide in the depth of the forest? But whether in the twilight or in the dark, in the thicket or in the jungle, on the mountain or on the moor, the voice can always be heard—and the voice is the principal medium 143 through which the sexes are brought into contact.

Well now, we come back to the question, why, if all species have a serviceable recognition call, that call should not be sufficient for the purpose, just as, without a doubt, it is adequate for all purposes at other seasons? The answer is, I think, clear. The recognition call is not confined to one sex, nor only to breeding birds; it is the common property of all the individuals of the species, and if the female were to rely upon it as a guide she might at one moment pursue another female, at another a non-breeding male; she might even be guided to a paired female or to a paired male, and time would be wasted and much confusion arise. So that no matter how much a male might advertise himself by cries and calls which were common alike to all the individuals of the species, it would not assist the biological end which we have in view. Something else is therefore required to meet the peculiar circumstances, some special sound bearing a definite meaning by which the female can recognise, amongst the host of individuals of no consequence to her, just those particular males in a position to breed and ready to receive mates. Hence the vocal powers, the power of producing sounds instrumentally, and the power of flight, have been organised to subserve the biological end of "recognition."

And this view is strengthened, it seems to me, by the erratic behaviour of certain species, 144 more particularly by one remarkable case, the case of the Cuckoo. The male, after having established himself, utters his call persistently from the day of arrival until approximately the middle of June; but, in contrast with the large majority of species, the female has a characteristic call which she, too, utters at frequent intervals. The female is polyandrous and has a sphere of influence embracing the territories of a number of males; she wanders from place to place, is often silent, and not unfrequently is engaged in dealing with her egg or in searching for a nest in which to deposit it, and therefore she is not always in touch with a male, still less with any particular one. Now there is much evidence to show that the discharge of the sexual function amongst birds is subject to control, and that this control operates through the female—through her physiological state becoming susceptible to stimulation only at certain periods. So that we have these considerations, that the female is polyandrous, that she has a territory distinct from that of the male, and that her sexual impulse is periodical; and the further consideration that the impulse, since it is periodical, is of limited duration and must receive immediate satisfaction. Such being the circumstances of the case, would the voice of the male serve to insure the union of the sexes at the appropriate moment? Well, the fact that she is polyandrous implies that every male in her sphere of influence is not always capable of satisfying her 145 sexual instinct. Is, then, the male's call an indication of his readiness to yield to stimulation? Without a doubt it is an index of the general physiological state which generates the sexual impulse, without a doubt it denotes a general preparedness to breed, but there is no evidence to show that it denotes the degree of ardour of the male at any particular moment, and much that proves the contrary. So that only by the female producing some special sound which will attract the males that are eager and bring them rapidly to the spot where she happens to be, only thus is it possible to insure the consummation of the sexual act. This, it seems to me, is the purpose of the peculiar call of the female—a call which, so far as biological interpretation is concerned, is just as much a song as the melody of the Marsh-Warbler—and its interest for us just now lies in this, that here we have a special case in which the sexes have separate territories, the female is polyandrous, and the voice of the male is not sufficient by itself to bring to pass the union of the sexes; and in which, consequently, if the purpose of song be that of recognition, we should expect to find, as we do find, that the female had a distinct and penetrating call.

We now come to the question of "warning," by no means the least important purpose of song. I pointed out that one of the chief differences between the call-notes and the song was that the former were socially serviceable, 146 whereas the latter was only serviceable to certain individuals; and in making this statement, I had in mind the direct benefits to the community which proceeded from an appreciation of sounds having a mutually beneficial meaning, not the indirect, though none the less beneficial, consequences to the species as a whole. Biologically considered, song, if it acts as a warning and thereby leads in one way or another to more complete success in the rearing of offspring, may be spoken of as socially serviceable; but it is legitimate to draw a distinction between the prospective value of remote relationships which we can foresee, and the mutual assistance which the individuals of a community derive from their close association.

If there were always sufficient breeding ground to support the offspring of all the individuals of each species, if the individuals were always so distributed that there was no possibility of overcrowding in any particular area, and if the conditions of existence of different species were so widely divergent that the presence of this one in no way affected the interests of that, no opportunity would be afforded for the development of so complex a system as is involved in the "territory" and all that appertains to it. But the available breeding ground is by no means unlimited. The supply of food, which is a determining factor in the environment, is always fluctuating according to the climate and according to the changes 147 in the earth's surface; and so the distribution of the bird population in any given area, though it may be suitably adjusted for one year or even for a period of years, is bound in the course of time to require readjustment. Now there cannot be readjustment without competition, nor competition without combat. But the appeal to physical force is only a means to an end, and, since no male can endure incessant warfare and the perpetual strain of always being on the alert, without experiencing such physical exhaustion as might affect his power of reproduction, its direct effect upon the combatants cannot be otherwise than harmful—in fact it is a necessary evil which for the good of the species must be kept strictly within bounds. Bearing in mind, then, these two facts, namely that the distribution of the males is never stable and that overmuch fighting may defeat the end in view, we can appreciate the importance of any factor which will lead to a more uniform distribution and at the same time insure security by peaceable means.

The proximate end of the male's behaviour is isolation—how is it to be obtained? If, after having occupied a territory, the bird were to remain silent, it would run the risk of being approached by rivals; if, on the other hand, it were merely to utter the recognition call of the species, it would but attract them. In neither case would the end in view be furthered, and isolation would solely depend upon alertness and the capacity to eject intruders. Supposing, 148 however, that the song, just as it serves to attract the females, serves to repel other males, a new element is introduced deserving of recognition; for those males that had established themselves would not only be spared the necessity of many a conflict, but they would be spared also the necessity of constant watchfulness, and so, being free to pursue their normal routine—to seek food, to rest, and, if migrants, to recover from the fatigue of the journey, they would be better fitted to withstand the strain of reproduction; and those that were still seeking isolation in an appropriate environment, instead of settling first here and then there only to find themselves forestalled, would avoid and pass by positions that were occupied, establishing themselves without loss of time in those that were vacant. Without the aid of something beyond mere physical encounter to regulate dispersal, it is difficult to imagine how in the short time at disposal anything approaching uniformity of distribution could be obtained. Hence, both in the direction of limiting combat, of insuring accommodation for the maximum number of pairs in the minimum area, and of conserving energy, the song, by conveying a warning, plays an important part in the whole scheme.

And if this be so, if the song repels instead of attracting, it follows that the more distinct the sounds, the less likelihood will there be of confusion; for supposing that different species were to develop similar songs, whole areas might 149 be left without their complement of pairs just because this male mistook the voice of that, and avoided it when there was no necessity for doing so. So that just as from the point of view of "recognition" each female must be able to distinguish the voice of its own kind, so likewise the warning can only be adequate providing that the sounds are specifically distinct. A point, however, arises here in regard to closely related forms. Some species require similar food and live under similar conditions of existence; they meet in competition and fight with one another; and, if they did not do so, the food-supply of a given area would be inadequate to support the offspring of all the pairs inhabiting that area. Generally speaking, the more closely related the forms happen to be, the more severe the competition tends to become; and it may be argued that in such cases a similar song would contribute to more effective distribution and in some measure provide against the necessity of physical encounter; that, in fact, it would stand in like relation to the success of all the individuals concerned, as does the song to the individuals of the same species. But we must bear in mind that the primary purpose of song is to direct the females to those males that are in a position to breed; and to risk the possibility of prompt recognition in order that the males of closely related species should fight the less, would be to sacrifice that which is indispensable for a more remote and less important advantage.

150 What meaning does the song convey to a male that is unestablished? Does the bird recognise that it is forestalled; does it foresee and fear the possibility of a conflict, and conclude that the attempt to settle is not worth while? I do not imagine that it thinks about it at all. How then does the warning warn? We will endeavour to answer this question, but, in order to do so, we must review the stages by which a territory is secured.

We take as our starting point the internal organic changes which are known to occur. These changes are correlated with other changes, manifested by a conspicuous alteration in behaviour—to wit, the disappearance of sociability and its replacement by isolation. Having found a station which meets the requirements of its racial characteristics, the male establishes itself for a season, becomes vociferous, displays hostility towards others of its kind, and in due course is discovered by a female. The whole is thus an inter-related whole, a chain of activities which follow one another in ordered sequence. Now we have seen that it is neither pugnacious nor vociferous until the territory is actually occupied; we have seen that the fact of occupation is the condition under which the instincts of pugnacity and of song are rendered susceptible to appropriate stimulation; we have discussed the nature of the stimulus in each case, and we wish to know the sort of meaning that the song conveys to an individual which is still in the preliminary stage of seeking a station. In 151 sequential order we have the following: (1) internal organic changes which lead to isolation, (2) the appropriate environment which gives rise to an impulse to remain in it, (3) the occupation of a territory which is the condition under which the instincts are rendered susceptible to stimulation, (4) the various stimuli. Each is dependent upon that which precedes it, and no part can be subtracted without failure of the biological end in view, neither can the different stages be combined in different order. So that, in considering the significance of song to an unestablished male, we are dealing with the situation at a point at which all the latent activities have not been fully felt, for all that so far has occurred is the change from sociability to isolation determined by internal organic changes. The bird has not established a territory because it has not come into contact with the appropriate environment, and it is not pugnacious because the condition which renders its instinct susceptible is absent; and so, as it wanders from place to place and hears the voices of males here or males there, it merely behaves in accordance with that part of its nature which predominates just at that particular moment—the impulse to avoid them.

But given the appropriate environment, given, that is to say, just that combination of circumstances which might bring into functional activity all the latent instincts of the intruder, and no matter how vociferous the occupant of a territory might be, it would not be preserved 152 from molestation. The advantage of the song, biologically considered, is then this, that it will often prove just sufficient to preclude males in search of isolation from coming into contact with the environmental conditions adequate to supply the stimulus to their latent activities and to convert them into rivals.

If this interpretation be correct, if we are right in attributing the withdrawal solely to the fact that the first stage only in the relational series has been reached, it follows that the effect of song upon males that have reached subsequent stages in that series must be of a very different kind. We have dealt with the male when in the preliminary stage of seeking isolation, we must deal with it now when eventually it occupies a territory. How does it behave when it hears, as it is bound to do, the voices of rivals in its neighbourhood? You may remember that some allusion was made to the fact that an outburst of song from one individual was followed, not unfrequently, by a similar outburst on the part of other individuals in the immediate locality. For example, silence may reign in the reed-bed except for an occasional note of the Reed-Warbler or Sedge-Warbler. Suddenly, however, a dispute arises between two individuals, accompanied by a violent outburst of song, and forthwith other males in the vicinity begin to sing excitedly and continue doing so for some minutes in a strangely vigorous manner, the tumult of voices affording a striking contrast to the previous silence. 153 Spasmodic outbursts of this kind, stimulated by an isolated utterance, are by no means uncommon. But not only does song stimulate song; under certain conditions it has the still more remarkable effect of arousing hostility. The boundary that separates two adjoining territories is by no means a definite line, but rather a fluid area wandered over by this owner at one moment, by that at another. Now so long as the bird is silent while in this area, the probability is that it will escape detection and remain unmolested; let it however sing—it often does so—and it will not merely be approached but attacked, and consequently this area is the scene of much strife. The point to be noticed here is that the song brings about no withdrawal; it elicits a response, attracts instead of repelling, and, in short, arouses the impulse that is always predominant in the nature of the male when eventually it occupies a territory—the impulse of self-assertiveness. Therefore it seems clear that the different stages in the process of reproduction mark the appearance of different conditions, each of which renders some new impulse susceptible to stimulation, and that the significance of song depends upon the stage which happens to have been reached. Hence when we speak of song acting as a "warning," we do not mean that it arouses any sensation of fear; it is but a stimulus to that part of the inherited nature of the hearer which predominates at the moment.

154 Are we then justified in the use of such terms as "warning," "significance," or even "meaning," when it is but a matter of stimulus and response? In what does the impulse to avoid other males consist? There is no reason to suppose that there is any sensation of fear in the first stage, and the course of behaviour demonstrates that there is none in the later stages. But it is difficult to conceive of an impulse which has, as its end, the isolation of the individual from members of its own sex and kind, without some feeling-tone, the reverse of pleasurable, entering into the situation; just as it is difficult to believe that the female experiences no pleasurable sensation when she hears the voice of the male that directs her search. So that the song may be actually repellent in the one case and attractive in the other; and it is none the less repellent when, as in the later stages, it attracts a neighbouring male, for the attraction is then of a different order, determined by the presence of the condition which renders the pugnacious nature susceptible and leads to attack. In a sense, therefore, we can speak of "meaning"—though not perhaps of "significance"—and of "warning," when we refer to the prospective value of the behaviour.

So much for the purpose of "song", there still remains the more difficult question—the question of origin. Let me make clear what I mean by origin. As we have already seen, there is infinite diversity in the sexual voice 155 of different species; some are harsh and others monotonous, and some strike the imagination by their novelty whilst others are melodious; and to the naturalist each, in its particular way and in a particular degree, probably makes some appeal according to the associations that it arouses. But just why a Marsh-Warbler is gifted with a voice that is so beautiful and varied, whilst the Grasshopper-Warbler must perforce remain content with a monotonous trill; just why the tail feathers of the Snipe have developed into an instrument, whilst the Pied Woodpecker has developed muscles which enable it to make use of a decayed branch as an instrument—we know no more than we do of the nature of the forces which lead the Reed-Warbler to weave its nest to reeds, or the caterpillar of the Elephant Hawk Moth to assume so peculiar an attitude when disturbed. When therefore I speak of the origin, I do not refer to the mode of origin of variation; I take for granted that variations somehow arise, and I seek to ascertain whether there is anything in the phenomena which we have explored which might reasonably be held to determine the survival of this one in preference to that.

When we reflect upon the problem of song and consider the numerous and diverse forms in which it is manifested, we are apt to draw a comparison between the sounds we hear and those produced by musical instruments, and hence to conclude that each bird is gifted 156 with a special instrument in virtue of which it produces its characteristic melody. But there is a very remarkable phenomenon connected with the singing of birds which shows that this is really not the case—I mean the phenomenon of imitation. There are plenty of good imitators amongst our native species, and the power of imitation is not the exclusive property of those which have reached a high degree of vocal development, nor, for the matter of that, of song-birds at all. Even the Jay, than which few birds have a more raucous voice, that "hoots" like the Wood-Owl, or copies the sounds produced by the tail feathers of the Snipe, will occasionally imitate the most melodious strains of some other species; and the Red-backed Shrike, whose sexual call is principally a few harsh notes rapidly repeated, bursts at times into perfect imitations of the song of the Swallow, Linnet, or Chaffinch. Nevertheless it is amongst such typical songsters as the Warblers that we find the greatest volume of imitation, and no limit seems to be placed upon their capacity. The Marsh-Warbler can utter the call of the Green Woodpecker, or sing as the Nightingale does, with as much facility as it sings its own song; and the Blackcap is well-nigh as proficient in copying the cries and melodies of surrounding species—and so, if it were necessary, we might proceed to add to the list.

These examples demonstrate that different songs are not represented by a corresponding 157 number of different physiological contrivances; for if the difference were really attributable to some structural peculiarity, then the range of sounds embraced in the call-notes and the sexual call of any given species, must be the measure of the capacity of its instrument; and no matter how great its power of imitation may be, it follows that it will only be capable of copying those sounds which fall within that range. There is plenty of evidence to show that the power of imitation is almost unlimited, at all events that it is not confined within such narrow limits as are here demanded. Hence it seems clear that the diversity of song is not to be sought in structure, but in some innate capacity to play one tune in preference to another; and if this be so, and if out of the same instrument, which has been primarily evolved to further the biological end of intercommunication, all manner of diverse sounds can be made to proceed, the problem of the origin of song is to that extent simplified.

We must next inquire into the nature of song, and endeavour to ascertain whether all the individuals of a species are alike proficient, or, failing this, whether there is any quality which can be observed to be constant under all conditions. I watch the Reed-Buntings in a marsh and find that there are three males occupying adjoining territories. Two of them are fully mature and their plumage is bright: that is to say the crown is black, the collar 158 and breast are white, the flanks are dull white spotted with black, and the mantle is reddish-brown. The third is immature: the crown, instead of being black, is suffused with brown; the collar, instead of being white, is mottled with brown; and the flanks are more heavily streaked with brown. These three birds take up their positions in February, and, as is their wont, sing incessantly each day at daybreak. The song of the first two is normal, including the usual number of phrases which flow in no definite sequence, but are combined and recombined in different order, and the tone is pure; that of the third, the immature bird, is, however, very different; for just as in comparison its plumage is dull, so the phrases of its song are limited and reiterated with great monotony, the tone is impure, and the whole performance is dull and to our ears unmusical. I watch them from February to June, and observe the order in which they are mated—first a mature male; next, after a short interval, the immature male; and finally, after a still longer interval, the remaining bird gets a mate. As the season advances, still keeping watch on the development of the plumage and of the voice of the immature male, I observe that no very definite change takes place—that the colours remain dull, that there is a conspicuous absence in the song of certain phrases, and that the notes lack purity of tone.

If now, instead of Reed-Buntings in a marsh, 159 I watch Yellow Buntings on a furze-covered common, I find that, establishing themselves early in February, they sing persistently, and in a few weeks are paired. But what arrests my attention more particularly is the quality of the song; for although the voice is unmistakably the voice of the Yellow Bunting, yet it is incomplete and lacks the variety of phrases and musical notation which we customarily associate with the bird. Nevertheless, as the season advances, there is a progressive development in both these directions, and by the end of March or the beginning of April the song possesses all those qualities which appeal to us so forcibly.

There is one other fact to which attention must be drawn—the variation in the song of the same species in different districts. As an illustration let us take the case of the Chaffinch. In Worcestershire the bird sings what I imagine to be a normal song—the notes are clear and the phrases are distinct and combined in numerous ways. With the notes fresh in mind I leave them and go to the west of Donegal, where I am at once conscious of a difference; not a subtle difference that perplexes the mind and is difficult to trace, but a change so remarkable that one is conscious of a passing doubt as to whether after all the voice is the voice of the Chaffinch; the song is pitched in a lower key, certain phrases are absent, the notes lack tone and are sometimes even harsh, and the bird seems wholly in 160 capable of reaching the higher notes to which I am accustomed.

Now the immature Reed-Bunting, though to our ears its song is but a poor representation of that of the adult, gains a mate; the Yellow Bunting pairs, and the discharge of the sexual function may even have taken place before its voice attains what we judge to be its full development; and there are no grounds for supposing that the Donegal Chaffinch, with its less musical notes, has on that account any the less chance of procreating its kind—facts which demonstrate that the biological value of song is neither to be sought in the purity of tone, nor in the variety and combination of phrases, nor, indeed, in any of those qualities by which the human voice gains or loses merit, and which leave us with no alternative but to dismiss from our minds all æsthetic considerations in the attempt to estimate its true significance.

What, then, determines its value? Are there any qualities which, whether the bird is mature or immature, whether it is untrained or has acquired fuller expression by practice, whether it inhabits this district or that, are alike constant? Well, no matter how great the variation, no matter how much this voice falls below or exceeds the standard, judged from the human standpoint, attained by that, even we, with our duller perception, have no difficulty in recognising the species to which the owner of the voice belongs; in other 161 words, the song is always specific, and this is the most noticeable, as it is the most remarkable, characteristic.

There is still, however, another quality to which I would draw attention—that of loudness. The sounds produced are on the whole alike penetrative, and the individuals of any given district, even though the climate by affecting their vocal muscles may have modified the character of the song, are at no disadvantage in this respect; neither are the females on the same account the less likely to hear the undeveloped voice of the immature male.

We have then the following considerations: firstly, there is the widespread and remarkable phenomenon of imitation, from which we can infer that the diversity of song is not due to structural differences but must be sought in some innate capacity to play one tune in preference to another; secondly, not all the individuals of the same species play a similar tune—we find that there is in certain directions a noticeable variation which nevertheless does not seem to affect the question of success or failure in the attainment of reproduction; in the third place, in contrast with this variation, we can observe a striking uniformity in two important particulars, namely in the specific character and penetrative power of the song—qualities which we know are essential for the purposes of "recognition" and "warning"; and finally, from the general course of our investi 162 gation, we can infer that if a male had no certain means of advertising its position, the territory would not be brought into useful relation in its life. Have we here sufficient ground on which to construct a theory of origin; in other words, has the evolution of song been incidental to, and contributory to, the evolution of the territory?

We have all along spoken of the song and of the call-notes as if they were manifestations of separate emotional states having their respective and well-defined spheres of usefulness; and while, speaking generally, this is a true statement of the case, there is much evidence to show that the relationship between them is nevertheless very close. There are, for example, quite a number of cases in which a particular call-note is uttered with unusual energy during sexual emotion, and is attached to the song, of which it may be said to form a part; but a still closer connection can be traced in many simple melodies which are merely compositions of social and family calls repeated many times in succession, and even in some of the more complex productions there will be found indications of a similar construction. And since this is so, since moreover, in the seasonal vocal development of such a bird as the Yellow Bunting, we can observe the gradual elaboration from simple to complex—from the repetition of single notes to phrases and from phrases to the complete melody—we have every reason to suppose that 163 it is along these lines that the evolution of the voice has proceeded.

In all probability there was a time when vocal expression was limited to primitive social and family cries which would be called into play with special force during times of excitement, more particularly during the sexual season which is the period of maximum emotional excitement. But the excitement would express itself in all the congenital modes of behaviour peculiar to the season, and thus the repetition of these cries would become associated with combat, with extravagant feats of flight, and with other forms of motor response. Now the more emotional individuals would be the more pugnacious, and all the more likely therefore to secure territory and so to procreate their kind; and, being of an excitable disposition, they would at the same time be the more vociferous. Hence variations of the hereditary tendency to vocal expression, even though in themselves they were not of survival value, would be fostered and preserved, so long as they were not harmful, in virtue of their association with pugnacity. But if, instead of being neutral, they helped to further the biological end of combat, the relationship between the voice and pugnacity would be of a mutually beneficial kind; and those individuals in which variation in both directions happened to coincide, would have a better chance of success in the attainment of reproduction.

A territorial system, closely corresponding 164 to that which we have discussed, forms part of the life behaviour of certain mammals, and of its existence much lower in the scale of life evidence is not wanting; from which we can infer that it is not of recent origin, but that the conditions in the external environment demanded such a system at a remote period of avian development. Now even in its incipient stages the system must have involved a separation of the sexes, and howsoever slight the degree of separation may have been in comparison with that which can be observed to-day, inasmuch as the power of locomotion was then less highly developed, mating could only have proceeded satisfactorily providing that males fit to breed had some adequate means of disclosing their positions. Thus there is reason to think that from the very commencement of the process variations of emotional disposition expressed through the voice would have been of survival value.

But expressed in what direction, in loudness and persistency of utterance, these are the qualities which, I imagine, would have been more likely to have facilitated the search of the female? Yet if she were uncertain as to the owner of the voice, neither loudness nor persistent repetition would avail much; and as species multiplied and the competition for the means of living became increasingly severe, so the necessity of a territory would have become intensified, and so, too, with the extension of range, would the separation of the sexes have 165 been an ever-widening one; and as with their multiplication, irregularities and delays in mating, arising from the similarity of the calls, would have increased in frequency, so a distinctive call, which would have tended to minimise these risks, would have come to possess biological value.

Here we have a theory of origin, but origin of what? Of certain characteristics of song—nothing more; and therefore to suppose that it furnishes a complete explanation, which satisfies all the requirements of scientific logic, of so wonderful an intonation as that, for example, of the Marsh-Warbler, or that no other relationships, except that of the territory, enter into the total emotional complex, simplifying here or elaborating there to meet the exigencies of diverse circumstances—to suppose this would be foolish. That there are many relationships which even to-day are leading to modifications in important particulars, but which at the present time are beyond our cognisance, of this there can be no doubt.

There is one process by which song may have attained a fuller development, and which would account in some measure for the elaboration, inexplicable merely in terms of "recognition." It is this: the effect of the sexual call upon the female cannot well be neutral, it must be either pleasurable or the reverse—it must, that is to say, be accompanied by some suggestiveness, and by suggestion I mean the arousing of some emotion akin to that of the male; and if there 166 are degrees of suggestiveness, which well there may be, some males will mate sooner than others and some will remain mateless—this is the theory of sexual selection. The question to be decided here is whether the biological emphasis is on loudness, or specific distinctness, or pitch, or modulation, or the manner in which the phrases are combined—that is, on some qualities in preference to others—or whether the emphasis is on the whole. We have already seen, and it is well known, that there is much variation in the voices of different individuals of the same species, and thus the first condition of the theory is fulfilled. Now the conditions which lead to variation are threefold—immaturity, seasonal sexual development, and isolation. Of the three, the variation in the case of the immature bird is the most instructive; the tone is not so pure, the combination of phrases is incomplete, and elaboration is imperfect, and yet, notwithstanding all these imperfections, we can observe that the bird pairs as readily as does the adult. But even if we lacked this demonstrative evidence, we should still be justified in assuming that such must be the case, for we know from experience in the preservation of game, where there is no surer way of reducing the stock than by leaving too high a percentage of old cocks, that for the young bird to be at any disadvantage in competition with the adult is detrimental, if not disastrous, to the species. So that while there is plenty of evidence of variation in those particular qualities which appeal to our æsthetic 167 faculties, there is at the same time evidence which demonstrates that such variations exercise no influence on the course of mating; and inasmuch as it is difficult to conceive of any voice departing more from the normal type in these particular qualities than the immature does from the adult, if there be degrees of suggestive influence, we must seek it in some other direction. There remain the two other characteristics which we found to be constant under all circumstances, namely, loudness and specific distinctness; and if, in addition to serving the purpose of disclosing the positions of the males, they serve to evoke some emotion in the female, which helps to further the biological end of mating, so much the more reason is there for their survival.

There can be no question that this ingenious and attractive theory, if it were true in its special application to song, would immensely simplify interpretation, and moreover that preferential mating would contribute not a little to the success of the whole territorial system. No one can deny the strength of the argument: that the sexual instinct, like all other instincts, must require a stimulus of an appropriate kind; that the effect of the sexual call upon the female cannot be neutral; and hence the probability that stimulation varies too; no one, I say, can question the strength of this evidence, and, one might add, of the evidence derived from the analogy of the human voice. But 168 when we have said this, we have said all; and our acceptance of the hypothesis, so far as song is concerned, must remain provisional so long as the evidence remains but secondary evidence.
169

CHAPTER V

THE RELATION OF THE TERRITORY TO THE SYSTEM OF REPRODUCTION

In the first two chapters I tried to show that the inherited nature of the male leads it to remain in a definite place at a definite season and to become intolerant of the approach of members of its own sex, and that a result is thus attained which the word "territory" in some measure describes. But the use of this word is nevertheless open to criticism, for it denotes a human end upon which the highest faculties have been brought to bear, and consequently we have to be on our guard lest our conception of the "territory" should tend to soar upwards into regions which require a level of mental development not attained by the bird. It is necessary to bear this in mind now we have come to consider the meaning of the territory, or rather the position that it occupies in the whole scheme of reproduction.

Relationship to a territory within the interrelated whole of a bird's life serves more than one purpose, and not always the same purpose in the case of every species. We have only 170 to glance at the life-histories of divergent forms to see that the territory has been gradually adjusted to suit their respective needs—limited in size here, expanded there, to meet new conditions as they arose. Now some may think that the theory would be more likely to be true if the territory had but one purpose to fulfil, and that one the same for every species; and they may see nothing but weakness in the multiplication of ways in which I shall suggest it may be serviceable. But such an objection, if it were raised, would arise from a mistaken conception, a conception which, instead of starting with a relationship and working up to the "territory," sees in the "territory" something of the bird's own selection and thence works back to its origin. Holding the view that it is nothing but a term in a complex relationship which has gradually become interwoven in the history of the individual, I see no reason why the fact of its serving a double or a treble purpose should not be a stronger argument for its survival. I now propose to examine the various ways in which the territory may have been of use in furthering the life of the individual, and the circumstances in the inorganic world which have helped to determine its survival.

The purpose that it serves depends largely upon the conditions in the external environment—the climate, the supply of food, the supply of breeding-stations, and the presence of enemies. Hence its purpose varies with 171 varying conditions of existence. But before we proceed to examine the particular ways in which it has been modified to suit the needs of particular classes of species, and the reason for such modifications, we must inquire whether there is not some way in which it has been serviceable alike to every species, or at least to a large majority of them.

Success in the attainment of reproduction depends upon the successful discharge of the sexual function; and the discharge of the sexual function depends primarily upon an individual of one sex coming into contact with one of the opposite sex at the appropriate season and when its appropriate organic condition arises. Now the power of locomotion is so highly developed in birds that it may seem unreasonable to suppose that males and females would have any difficulty in meeting when their inherited nature required that they should do so, still less reasonable to suggest that this power might even act as a hindrance to successful mating. Nevertheless, if we try to picture to ourselves the conditions which would obtain if the movements of both sexes were in no wise controlled, and mating were solely dependent upon fortuitous gatherings, we shall come, I fancy, to no other conclusion than that much loss of valuable time and needless waste of energy would often be incurred in the search, and that many an individual would fail to breed just because its wanderings took it into districts in which, at the time, there happened 172 to be too many of this sex or too few of that. And as the power of locomotion increased and the distribution of the sexes became more and more irregular, so the opportunity would be afforded for the development of any variation which would have tended to facilitate the process of pairing, and by so doing have conferred upon the individuals possessing it, some slight advantage over their fellows.

What would have been the most likely direction for variation to have taken? Any restriction upon the freedom of movement of both sexes would only have added to the difficulties of mating; but if restriction had been imposed upon one sex, whilst the other had been left free to wander, some order would have been introduced into the process. That the territory serves to restrict the movements of the males and to distribute them uniformly throughout all suitable localities, there can be no question; and since the instinctive behaviour in relation to it is timed to appear at a very early stage in the seasonal sexual process, the males are in a position to receive mates before the impulse to mate begins to assert itself in the female.

We will take the Ruff as an example. According to Mr. Edmund Selous, pairing, in this species, is promiscuous—the Ruffs are polygamous, the Reeves polyandrous. Suppose, then, that upon this island of some few miles in circumference, whereon his investigations were made, the movements of neither Ruff 173 nor Reeve were subject to control, that the birds wandered in all directions, and that the union of the sexes were fortuitous, would the result have been satisfactory? We must remember that the Reeve requires more than one Ruff to satisfy her sexual instinct; we must also bear in mind the possibility that the functioning of her instinct may be subject to some periodicity, and we ask whether, under these circumstances, accidental gatherings would meet all the requirements of the situation. Now, manifestly, she must be in a position to find males when her appropriate organic condition arises. But in the absence of any system in the distribution of the sexes, how could delay be avoided, or how could a uniform discharge of the sexual function be assured? There is, however, a system. In the first place, there are the assembly grounds to which the birds repair season after season; and then, on the assembly grounds, there are the territories, represented, as Mr. Selous tells us, by depressions where the grass by long use has been worn away, and each depression is owned by one particular Ruff. The assembly grounds have the effect of splitting up and scattering the birds, and the number of Ruffs at any one particular meeting place is limited by the territories; with the result that Ruffs fit to breed are evenly distributed and always to be found in certain definite places, and the Reeves know by experience where to find them.

The advantage of this territorial system is 174 therefore apparent. Instead of this district being overcrowded and that one deserted; instead of there being too many of one sex here and too few of the other sex there; instead of a high percentage of individuals failing to procreate their kind, just because circumstances over which they have no control prevent their discovering one another at the appropriate time—each sex has its allotted part to play, each district has its allotted number of inhabitants, and the waste of energy and the loss of time incurred in the process of mating is reduced to a minimum.

Let us return again to the question of fortuitous mating, and consider the position of a male and female that have discovered one another by accident and have paired; what will be the subsequent course of their behaviour? We are assuming, of course, that a territory forms no part of their life-history. If the discharge of the sexual function takes place immediately and the ovaries of the female are in an advanced state of seasonal development, the construction of the nest will proceed without delay—and the nest will answer the same purpose as the territory in so far as it serves to restrict the movements of the birds and tends to make them remain in, or return to, its vicinity; but if not, there will be an interval during which both sexes will continue to wander as before, guided only by the scarcity or abundance of food. In the first case, there will be the attraction of the nest to prevent any untimely 175 separation; in the second, there will be nothing in the external environment to induce them to remain in any particular spot. Now if we turn to any common species and observe the sequence of events in the life of different pairs, we shall find that pairing is seldom followed by an immediate attempt to build; that an interval of inactivity is the rule rather than the exception, and that this interval varies in different species, in different individuals, and in different seasons. Our imaginary male and female will therefore be faced with considerable difficulty; for with nothing in the external environment to attract them and with no restriction imposed upon the direction or extent of their flight, their union will continue to be, as it began by being, fortuitous. Next, let us consider their position were a disposition to establish a territory to form part of the inherited nature of the male. Each one will then be free to seek food when and where it wills and to associate with other individuals without the risk of permanent separation from its mate; and, no matter how long an interval may elapse between mating and nest-building, each one will be in a position to find the other when the appropriate moment for doing so arrives. Hence, while preserving freedom of movement for each individual, the territory will render their future, as a pair, secure.

No doubt the course of behaviour, as we observe it to-day in the lives of many species, is the outcome of, rather than the condition which 176 has led to, the evolution of the territory. Thus, in many cases, we find that early mating is the rule rather than the exception; we find that the sexes frequently separate to seek their food, and fly away temporarily in different directions; and, under exceptional climatic conditions, we find that they even revert to their winter routine and form flocks; only, however, to return to their territories, as pairs, under more congenial conditions. Yellow Buntings, for example, pair comparatively early in the season—some in the latter part of February, others in March, and others again in April; and some build their nests in April, others in May. There is a gorse-covered common which I have in mind, a favourite breeding resort of this species. Between this common and the surrounding country, the birds constantly pass to and fro. If you watch a particular male you will observe that it sings for a while in its territory, that it then rises in the air and disappears from view, and finally that it returns to the tree, bush, or mound which constitutes its headquarters, where it again sings. Meanwhile the female, with which there is every reason to believe that this male has paired, behaves similarly; she, too, flies to the surrounding country and in time returns with equal certainty. Sometimes male and female accompany one another—that is, they leave simultaneously and likewise return; at other times, though they depart together, the male returns alone; or the male may disappear in one direction whilst the female does so in 177 another—and, on the whole, there is a sameness in the direction of flight taken by the same pairs on different occasions. An interval of nearly two months may thus elapse between mating and nest-building, during which the sexes are not only often apart but often separated by a considerable distance.

What does this species gain by the individuals belonging to it mating so early in the season? If the appropriate condition which leads the females to seek males were to arise in each individual at a late date, the first stage in the process—mating—would not be completed before the second—the discharge of the sexual function—were due to begin. Thus, instead of having ample time, the females would have but a short period in which to discover males; and this in some cases might lead to delay, in others to failure, and in others again to needlessly severe competition, entailing physical exhaustion at a critical moment in their lives. Hence those females in which the appropriate organic condition developed early in the season would not only be more likely to find males, but would be in a position to rear more broods than those in which it developed late; and they would have a better chance of leaving offspring, which, in their turn, would reproduce the peculiarities of their parents. Moreover, within certain limitations, the more these successful females varied in the date of their development, the less severe would be the competition, and 178 the more uniformly successful would the mating of all the individuals in a given district tend to become. But all of this renders an interval of sexual inactivity unavoidable; an interval which must constitute a danger unless there were something in the external environment to prevent the male and female from drifting apart. Inasmuch, then, as the occupation of a territory serves to remove all possibility of permanent separation, I suggest that its evolution has afforded the condition under which this beneficial procedure has developed—free to mate when they will, free to seek food where they will, free to pursue their normal routine of existence, and to meet all exigencies as they arise in their ordinary daily life—whilst free to do this, their future, as a pair, is nevertheless secure.

Thus far we have considered the territory in its relation to the discharge of the sexual function. In many of the lower forms of life, the success or the failure of reproduction, so far as the individual is concerned, may be said to end with the completion of the sexual act—the female has but to deposit her eggs in a suitable environment and then her work is done, because in due course and under normal conditions of temperature the young hatch out, and from the first are able to fend for themselves. And so, when we come to consider the question of reproduction in the higher forms of life, we are apt to focus attention too much upon the sexual function and too little upon the con 179 tributary factors, the failure of any one of which would mean failure of the whole. For a bird, success in the attainment of reproduction does not merely imply the successful discharge of the sexual function; much more is demanded; it must find somewhere to build its nest and to lay its eggs, it must shield its young from extremes of temperature and protect them from enemies, and it must be in a position to supply them with food at regular intervals. And, consequently, every situation is not equally favourable for rearing young; there must be a plentiful supply of food of the right kind in the immediate vicinity of the nest, and it must be in greatest abundance just at the moment when it is most urgently needed—that is to say, during the first few weeks after the birth of the young. Success, therefore, depends upon manifold relationships which centre in the station, and these relationships vary in intensity with the conditions of existence.

First, then, let us examine the problem from the point of view of the foodsupply. There are many species whose success in rearing offspring is largely dependent upon the rapidity with which they can obtain food; and it makes but little difference which species we choose out of many—Finch, Bunting, Warbler, or Chat. I shall choose the Buntings, as their life-history in broad outline conforms to the general type, and, moreover, their behaviour is fresh in my mind. The young are born in a very helpless state; they are without covering 180 —fragile organisms, illfitted, one would think, to withstand extremes of temperature, and wholly incapable of protecting themselves from enemies of any description. For the first three days after they are hatched the female spends much of her time in brooding them, and, when she is thus occupied, the male sometimes brings food to her, which she proceeds to distribute or swallows. But all the young cannot be fed, neither are they ready to be fed, at the same moment; and the parents have besides to find food for themselves, and the nest has to be cleaned—all of which necessitates the young being exposed to the elements at frequent intervals. Now it is impossible to observe the instinctive routine of the parents, when the young need attention, without being impressed with the conative aspect of their behaviour. Why, we ask, are the movements of the female so brisk; why does she seek food and clean the nest so hurriedly; why, if her instinctive routine is interrupted, do her actions and her attitude betray such bewilderment? I take it that the only answer we can give to these questions is that the part of her inherited nature which predominates just at this particular time is to brood. But why is brooding of such importance? Partly to maintain the young at the proper temperature, and thereby to induce sleep—and sleep for offspring newly hatched is as important as food—and partly to protect them from the risk of exposure to extremes of temperature. This latter danger 181 is no imaginary one. Examine a young bird that has recently left the egg; observe its nakedness; and consider what it has to withstand—a temperature that may rise to 70° F. or may fall to 40° F., the tropical rain of a thunderstorm or the persistent drizzle of many hours' duration, the scorching effect of a summer sun or the chilling effect of a cold north-easterly wind, and, constantly, the sudden change of temperature each time that the parent leaves the nest. One marvels that it ever does survive; one marvels at the evolution of a constitution sufficiently elastic to withstand such changes. But, however much the constitution may give us cause to wonder, it is clear that much depends upon the parents. A slight inefficiency of the instinctive response which the presence of the young evokes, a little slowness in searching for food or sluggishness in returning to the nest, might lead to exposure and prove fatal. And, however much is demanded of the parents, it is clear that much also depends upon the relationships in the external environment; for no matter how sensitive or how well attuned the instinctive response of the parent may be, it will avail but little in the presence of unfavourable conditions in the environment.

Everything turns upon the question of the effect of exposure. And in order to ascertain how far extremes of temperature are injurious, I removed the nests of various species containing newly hatched young, and, placing them 182 in surroundings that afforded the customary amount of protection from the elements, I made a note of the temperature and the atmospheric conditions and then observed the condition of the young at frequent intervals. Details of these experiments will be found at the end of the chapter.

The experiments with the Blackbirds and the Whitethroats gave the most interesting results. Both broods of each species were respectively of much the same age, yet one brood of Blackbirds survived for five, and the other only for two and a half hours, and one brood of Whitethroats lived for twelve hours whilst the other succumbed in a little over an hour. This difference is rather remarkable; and it seems clear that the power of resistance of the young diminishes rapidly when the temperature falls below 52° F. It must be borne in mind, however, that the conditions under which the experiments were made were, on the whole, favourable—the weather was dry, the temperature was not unusually low, nor was the wind exceptionally strong or cold; and even in those cases in which the young succumbed so rapidly, the atmospheric conditions could by no means be regarded as abnormal.

What, then, would happen in an unusually wet or cold breeding season? For how long would the young then survive? In the spring and early summer of the year 1916, I was fortunate in observing the effect of exposure under natural but inclement conditions. I happened to be watching the Yellow Buntings on Hartlebury Common—200 acres of Upper Soft Red Sandstone, profusely overgrown with cross-leaved heath (*Erica tetralix*), ling (*Calluna vulgaris*), and furze (*Ulex*)—in one corner of which eight males had established adjoining territories covering some fifteen acres of ground. The males obtained mates towards the end of March or at the beginning of April; nests were built in the middle of May, and the successful pairs hatched out their young in June. On the 10th June the weather became exceptionally cold, and during the next ten days the temperature fell at times to 40° F. during the daytime. Slight frosts were registered at night in the district, and the young bracken, which covered the Common in places, had the appearance of having been scorched and eventually withered away. At the coldest period of this cold spell the young were hatched in two of the nests—in the first one on the 10th June, and in the second a day or so later; and on the morning of the 10th June, having found a suitable position near the first nest, I began to watch the movements of the parents, with the intention of keeping some record of their behaviour each day so long as the young needed attention. An hour passed without their appearing, and on examining the young I found that they were cold, feeble, and unresponsive, but the female presently arrived and went to the nest. Later in the day the young were lively and responded freely when the nest was approached, but nevertheless I was impressed with the length of time during which the parents were absent; for, judging by the experience of previous experiment, there seemed to be every likelihood of their losing their offspring in such abnormally cold weather, unless they brooded them more persistently. On the 11th June at 5.50 A.M. neither parent was to be seen and the young could scarcely be made to respond; but shortly afterwards both male and female appeared, and, after remaining a few minutes, again disappeared without even approaching the nest. At 6.45 A.M. no attempt had been made to brood and the young were then so feeble that they were scarcely able to open their mouths, and at 6 P.M. one was still alive but the remaining three were dead. Yet the parents returned and the female went to the nest; and, from a distance of a few feet, I watched her brooding the living and the dead. At 5.45 A.M. the following day the remaining young bird had succumbed, the temperature then being 49° F.

At the second nest, I was unable to watch the behaviour of the parents so closely. On the 15th June the nest contained three young from three to four days old, and during the morning of that and the succeeding day nothing unusual occurred, with the exception that the period of exposure seemed, as in the former case, to be too long. On the 17th June at 3.10 A.M. the young had collapsed and were stiff, but the parents were in their territory and anxious apparently to attend to their brood. At 9.15 A.M. only two of the young were left in the nest, and though I searched amongst the undergrowth and in the gorse bush in which the nest was placed, no trace of the third bird was to be found. Of the two remaining young, one was alive and responsive but the other was dead, and though the female attended assiduously to the sole surviving offspring, yet it too had succumbed by the following morning.

In a third territory, there was a nest containing four eggs. These eggs were due to hatch at much the same time as those in the two nests just referred to, but they failed to do so, and an examination showed that they contained well developed but dead chicks.

To what can the death of the young and of the chicks in the eggs be attributed? Not to any failure in the instinctive response of the females, for they fed their young, they brooded them, they even brooded the dead as well as the living, and probably did all that racial preparation had fitted them to do. Yet the fact that the young in the second nest were lifeless and exposed at 3 A.M. seems to betoken absence on the part of the parents during the night, and may be interpreted as a failure of the parental instinctive response. Let us return for a moment to the experiments. These showed, it will be remembered, that a rise or fall in the temperature of but a few degrees was sufficient to make an astonishing difference in the length of time that the young were able to survive without their parents; that when the temperature reached 58° F. the bodies of the young retained their warmth, and that under such conditions even a night's exposure had little, if any, effect; so that even supposing that the parents were absent during the night, the death of the young cannot be said to have been due to a failure of the parental instinct, because under normal conditions—and under such has their instinctive routine been evolved—their absence would not have prejudiced the existence of the offspring. I attribute the collapse of the young solely to the exceptional cold that prevailed at just the most critical time, and I base this conclusion partly on the experience gained from experiment, but mainly on their condition observed at different intervals; for during exposure they collapsed rapidly, their flesh became cold and their movements sluggish, their response grew weak, and gradually they became more and more feeble until they could scarcely close their bills after the mandibles had been forced asunder. Yet, even after having reached so acute a stage of collapse, the warmth from the body of the brooding bird was sufficient to restore them temporarily; once more they would become lively and responsive, only, however, to revert to the previous condition soon after the parent had again abandoned them. Doubtless their power of resistance grew less and less during each successive period of exposure.

If the nestling Bunting is to be freed from the risk of exposure, it is evident that there 187 must be, in the vicinity of the nest, an adequate supply of food upon which the parents can draw liberally. Hence those pairs that exercise dominion over the few acres surrounding the nest, and are thus able to obtain food rapidly, will stand a better chance of rearing their offspring than others which have no certain supply to draw upon—and this, I believe, is one of the biological ends for which the territory has been evolved. But it must not be supposed that each pair finds, or even attempts to find, the whole of the food within its territory, or that it is necessary for the theory that it should do so; all that is required is that such overcrowding as might lead to prolonged absence on the part of the parents and inordinate exposure of the young shall be avoided. So that the problem has to be considered not merely from the point of view of the individual, but from the larger point of view of all the pairs inhabiting a given area.

Now there were eight pairs of Yellow Buntings occupying the one corner of Hartlebury Common, and their territories in the aggregate covered some fifteen acres. The birds obtained part of their food-supply amongst the gorse and in some young scattered oak-trees, and part in an adjoining coppice and on the surrounding arable land. But they were not the sole occupants of this corner of the Common; other insectivorous species had territories there also—amongst which were Whitethroats, Grasshopper-Warblers, Willow-Warblers, 188 Whinchats, Stonechats, Meadow-Pipits, Tree-Pipits, and Skylarks. Suppose then that there had been sixteen pairs of Yellow Buntings instead of eight; that there had been other pairs, which assuredly there were, inhabiting the locality; that they had also resorted, which assuredly they did, to the coppice and arable ground for the purpose of securing food; and that their numbers had also been increased in a similar ratio—would a supply of food for all have been forthcoming with the necessary regularity and promptitude? Well, the parents might have had to travel a little farther; but even if they had been compelled to do so, their absence would only have been prolonged by so many minutes the more, and under normal conditions what harmful result to the offspring could possibly have followed? The question for us, however, is not what might have occurred under normal conditions, but whether the life behaviour is so adjusted as to meet the exigencies of diverse, and in this case of abnormal, circumstances. Now the capacity of the young to resist exposure diminishes very rapidly when the temperature falls below the normal—the danger zone seems to be reached at approximately 52° F., and the length of time during which they survive then becomes astonishingly short—and moreover the fall in the temperature would tend to decrease the supply of insect life upon which they depend, so that if the size of the territories had been reduced by one half, and the parents in consequence had been compelled to seek their 189 food at a greater distance, can it be doubted that the cumulative effect of even a few minutes of additional exposure would have been detrimental, if not disastrous, to the offspring?

We speak, however, of the parents extending their journeys a little farther in this direction or a little farther in that, as though they could do so with impunity except in so far as it affected themselves, or their offspring, or the other Yellow Buntings inhabiting that particular area. But, most certainly, any extension would have meant so much encroachment upon the available means of support of other members of the species inhabiting adjoining areas, whose young in turn would have been liable to have been affected; and, with even greater certainty, the Whitethroats, the Stonechats, the Tree-Pipits, and the Willow-Warblers that had also established themselves in that one corner of the Common would have been hard pressed to find sufficient food with sufficient rapidity.

Let me give another illustration of a somewhat different kind. Lapwings, as we saw in the previous chapters, establish territories and guard them from intrusion with scrupulous care. The young are able to leave the nest soon after they are hatched, and consequently the parents are not necessarily obliged to bring food *to* them—they can, if they so choose, lead them *to* the food. Whether each pair limits its search for food to its territory, I do not know. But even supposing that all ownership of territory were to lapse directly the young were hatched, 190 that the boundaries were to cease to exist, and that the birds were free to wander at will without fear of molestation, the end for which the territory had been evolved would none the less have been obtained; for inasmuch as the parents are accompanied by their young, it matters not in what part of the meadow they seek their food; all that matters is that the number of families shall not exceed the available supply of food. So far, then, as the Lapwing is concerned, the territory fulfils its purpose when once it limits the number of males, since, by doing so, it limits the number of families and prevents undue pressure upon the means of support.

Nevertheless, there are many birds that seem to rely entirely upon the territory to supply them with all that is necessary. Each Warbler seeks its food within the precincts of its own particular domain, and, except in occasional instances, neither resorts to neutral ground nor makes excursions into the locality immediately surrounding the territory, as does the Bunting. Probably it would be disastrous if it attempted to do so, for since its young at birth are so delicate and so susceptible to changes of temperature, it cannot afford to be absent from them for long. Of the two experiments made with young Whitethroats, one was made under favourable and the other under unfavourable conditions. In this latter case the temperature was 50° F., and the young, it may be remembered, only survived for a 191 little over one hour. Now exposure at that temperature is evidently dangerous, but it would be still more dangerous if the weather were wet instead of dry, and the temperature 46° F. instead of 50° F.; and it is, I imagine, on this account that the impulse to brood is so strongly implanted in the female. No sooner, it seems, does she depart than she returns with a small quantity of food which she hurriedly distributes and immediately settles down to brood; and if forcibly prevented from returning, her attitude betrays symptoms of what, humanly speaking, we should term great distress. If, then, the conditions in the external environment were such as would make it difficult for the female to obtain food rapidly, what advantage would she derive from so strongly developed an impulse? Might it not be a disadvantage? Might it not mean that she would abandon the search too readily and be content to return with an insufficient supply, and might not that be as injurious to the young as prolonged exposure? Manifestly the impulse to brood could only have developed strength in so far as it fitted in with all the other factors that make for survival; and the principal factor in the external environment seems to be the territory. How could the young have been freed from the risk of exposure if the impulse to brood had not been so strongly implanted in the parent? How could the impulse to brood have been free to develop if a supply of food had not 192 been first insured? How could the supply of food have been insured if numbers of the same species had been allowed to breed in close proximity?

From the foregoing facts it is clear that the young of many species are at birth susceptible to cold and unable to withstand prolonged exposure. The parents must therefore be in a position to obtain food rapidly, and consequently it is important that there should be an ample supply in the vicinity of the nest. This end the territory certainly serves to promote; it roughly insures that the bird population of a given area is in proportion to the available means of subsistence, and it thus reduces the risk of prolonged exposure to which the young are always liable.

This leads on to a consideration of those cases in which the question of securing food is subordinate to the question of securing a station suitable for reproduction.

I take the Guillemot as an example. In principle its behaviour is similar to that of the Bunting; the male repairs to a definite place, isolates itself, and becomes pugnacious. But the Guillemot is generally surrounded by other Guillemots, and the birds are often so densely packed along the ledges that there is scarcely standing room, so it seems, for all of them. Nevertheless the isolation of the individual is, in a sense, just as complete as that of the individual Bunting, for each one is just as 193 vigilant in resisting intrusion upon its few square feet as the Bunting is in guarding its many square yards, so that the evidence seems to show that that part of the inherited nature which is the basis of the territory is much the same in both species. What we have then to consider is, What is the biological value to the Guillemot of an inherited nature which, for the Bunting, has utility in relation to the supply of food for the young? Up to a point, the act of securing a territory has like value for each respective species, whether the area occupied be large or small—that is to say, it enables the one sex to discover the other with reasonable promptitude.

For the greater part of the year, Guillemots live at sea; singly, in twos or threes, or in small parties, they move upon the face of the waters, extending their wanderings far away from land, out into the broad ocean, where for weeks together they face the gales and heavy seas of the Atlantic. But in due course and in response to internal organic changes, they return, like the Warbler, to their breeding grounds—rocky headlands or islands appropriately situated and affording the appropriate rock formation. During all these months of wandering, the majority seem to ignore the land, to pass away from it altogether, and to spread themselves over the surface of the ocean regardless of mainland or island. Some useful observations, which throw some light on the distance that Guillemots are accustomed to 194 wander from land, were made by Lieut. B. R. Stewart during a number of voyages between various ports in Great Britain and Ireland and ports in North America, principally New York and Quebec. Thus, on the 24th March, large numbers were seen in lat. 55° N., long. 24° W., five hundred miles approximately from land, though on the following day—four hundred miles off Tory Island—they were not so plentiful. Again, on the 1st October, in lat. 53° N., long. 27° W., seven hundred miles or so from land, one bird was seen, whilst on the following day, in lat. 52° N., long. 21° W., a single individual was washed on board by the heavy seas and seemed little the worse for the adventure. Within two hundred miles of the west coast of Ireland, he found them plentiful on various occasions. From this it is clear that the circumstances under which the bird lives for many months in succession must impose a considerable strain upon its constitution; and how it is able to withstand the buffeting of wind and water, to secure its food, and to endure, is a mystery. It is important, therefore, that the young bird should be properly nourished and protected from anything that might harm its constitution, and important, too, that the parents should be freed from any undue strain during the course of reproduction.

The conditions which the breeding station has to fulfil are threefold: in the first place, it must be in proximity to the food-supply; secondly, it must provide the necessary shelter 195 for the egg and for the helpless offspring; and, in the third place, it must be so situated that the young can reach the water in safety. We will examine these conditions one by one.

The proximity to the food-supply is a consideration of some importance. The life of the Guillemot during the winter is a strenuous one; we know that large numbers succumb in stormy weather, and we can infer that slight constitutional defects might make all the difference between failure and success; and, therefore, the less severely the constitution of the parent is taxed during reproduction, and the more securely the constitution of the offspring is built up, the greater prospect will both have of resisting the hardships of the winter successfully. Much, then, will depend upon the distance the parents have to travel in order to obtain food. The farther the breeding station is removed from the feeding ground the greater the physical strain which will be imposed upon the birds, and the greater the chance will there be of the offspring being improperly nourished. Now the food consists of small fish, largely of sand-eels, which are secured in deep water, and the abundance of which varies, possibly according to the nature of the currents. Hence cliffs which are situated away from the water, or from which the water recedes at low tide, or which are surrounded by an area of shallow water, and are thus not in proximity to the feeding ground, even though 196 they may fulfil the second and third condition, will not answer the requirements of a breeding station.

Of no less importance is the type of rock-formation. Not every formation affords the necessary ledges upon which the egg can be deposited with safety—the face of the cliff may be too smooth, or too jagged, or the shelves may run at too acute an angle. Many of the large assemblages of Guillemots in the British Islands are found where the rock is quartzite, mica-schist, limestone, or chalk. The reason of this is that such rocks are weathered along the planes of stratification, of jointing, of cleavage, or of foliation—the strata being probably of unequal durability—with the result that innumerable shelves, ledges, and caverns, which are taken advantage of by the birds, form a network over the face of the cliff. But only those ledges can be made use of which are placed at a considerable height above the water, because, when the cliff faces the open sea, the lower ones are liable to be washed in stormy weather by the incoming swell and thus become untenable. There is a small cove in the midst of the most precipitous part of the breeding station at Horn Head, wherein the shingly shore shelves rapidly to the Atlantic and faces to the west. Here, towards the end of July, young Kittiwake Gulls can sometimes be found washed up on the beach—some living, but in every stage of exhaustion, others dead, and in every stage of decomposition; here is the young 197 bird, recently caught by the swell and thrown upon the shore, lying side by side with the remains of others that had previously succumbed to starvation—on every side evidence of the devastation wrought by the Atlantic. May not some of this destruction have been brought about by the nests having been placed upon the lower ledges within reach of an exceptionally heavy sea? Hence much depends upon the nature of the rock-formation, and many a mighty precipice, even though it may fulfil the first and third condition, is nevertheless valueless as a breeding station.

Finally, the young bird must occupy a ledge from which it can reach the water in safety. There is much difference of opinion as to the manner in which it leaves the ledge, but all agree that it does so before it is capable of sustained flight. If, then, the face of the cliffs were made up of a series of broken precipices, or if the rocks at the base projected out into the water, or if detached rocks abounded in the waters beneath, the mortality amongst the chicks would no doubt be considerable.

The coast-line of Co. Donegal will illustrate the foregoing remarks. On the southern and western side of the Slieve League promontory there is no real Guillemot station; only on the northern side—the quartzite in the vicinity of Tormore—are the birds to be found in large numbers. Northwards from here, a wild and rugged coast is passed over before other stations are reached—at the eastern end of Tory Island 198 and on Horn Head; and beyond this, to the east, there are none, not even on the old rocks that form the promontory of Inishowen. Why, we ask, do countless numbers crowd the ledges of Horn Head, whilst they are absent from the precipices of Slieve League; why, too, are they absent from the granite cliffs of Owey? The reason is not far to seek. Either the face of the cliff is made up of a series of broken precipices, or the face of the precipices is too smooth, or the otherwise suitable ledges are situated too near the water, or the water recedes from the base of the cliff at low tide. Many miles of rock-bound coast are thus useless for the purpose of reproduction.

Now when we bear in mind how large an expanse of coast is formed of blown sand or of rocks of low altitude, and how many miles of cliff fail to supply the three essential conditions that we have been considering, we can see that suitable breeding stations must be limited both in number and extent. From a wide expanse of ocean hosts of individuals are therefore obliged to converge at certain definite points; and hence, each recurring season, there must arise a competition for positions at the station, just as there is competition between individual Buntings for positions in the marsh. And the ability to obtain a position upon a suitable ledge involves, in the first place, an impulse to search for it; in the second place, an impulse to dwell in it; and in the third place, an impulse to resist intrusion 199 upon it. It would be useless for an individual to be pugnacious if it had no fixed abode; equally useless for it to establish itself on a particular ledge if it had no power to defend it—all of which implies an inherited nature similar to that of the Bunting. But the proximate end to which the competition is directed is not alike in the case of both species. In the case of the Guillemot it has reference solely to the piece of rock whereon the egg is laid; in the case of the Bunting to a piece of ground capable of furnishing an adequate supply of food for the young; and the reason for the difference is this, that there is always an abundance of food in the water beneath the cliff, but breeding stations are scarce, whereas there is always an abundance of situations in the marsh in which the Bunting can place its nest, but the supply of food varies and at times can only be obtained with difficulty.

If then the Guillemot were to behave after the manner of the Bunting and assign to itself a portion of the face of the cliff, or if it were only to occupy a few ledges, or an even lesser area—a single ledge—what would be the result? That it would attain to reproduction is beyond question; that the egg would be safely deposited there can be no manner of doubt; neither is there any reason to suppose that the offspring would not be successfully reared. But, indirectly, its behaviour would affect the Guillemot race. For if it be true, as the crowded ledges certainly seem to show, that there is a dearth of 200 suitable breeding ground, no greater calamity could befall the species than that some members should exercise dominion over too large an area of the habitable part of the cliff and thus prevent others from breeding. Under such conditions the race could not endure, since in this, as in every case, its survival must depend upon a close correspondence between the behaviour of the individual and the circumstances in the external environment.

Scarcity of suitable cliffs is the principal reason of the ledges being so closely packed with Guillemots, just as it accounts for this part of the precipice being crowded with Kittiwake Gulls, that part with Herring-Gulls, and that part again with Razorbills and Puffins. Yet each individual preserves its few square feet of rock or soil from molestation, and the area each one occupies varies according to the conditions of existence of the species. Thus the Herring-Gull occupies a comparatively small area, although one many times larger than that of the Guillemot. It requires more space than the latter, owing to the fact that it not only builds a nest but rears four instead of a single offspring, and it can be allowed this, because, since its young remain in the nest until they are capable of sustained flight, it can make use of many miles of cliff from which the tide recedes at the base, or which have, at their base, rocks jutting out into the sea; but manifestly it cannot be allowed so much space as the Bunting.

201 Martins build in close proximity to one another, owing probably to shortage of accommodation, and, in their case, the nests have to be so situated as to be sheltered from the wet. If water drips upon them for any length of time, the mud, of which they are composed, crumbles and large pieces fall away, with the result that the eggs or the young are precipitated to the ground. Consequently, not every house or perpendicular cliff will answer the purpose of a breeding station. A few pairs build their nests beneath the eaves close against the walls of my house, and year after year the result is much the same; after every downfall of rain, the water collects into rivulets, trickles down over the eaves, is absorbed by the mud and destroys the nests. Thereupon, the birds set to work and rebuild; but again the nest is destroyed, and again they rebuild, and so on throughout the summer, and only on rare occasions do they succeed in rearing offspring at the proper season. Similar conditions must prevail in many situations; but, clearly, the more binding and plastic the building material, the longer the nest will withstand the action of the dripping water and the greater chance will there be of the young being reared in safety. Observe, therefore, how far-reaching an effect so small a detail as the nature of the mud can have upon the status of the species in any given locality. Where the conditions are favourable, there the birds must congregate to breed, and, like the Guillemot, if each individual exercised 202 dominion over too large an area, the species as a whole would suffer.

In all these examples, the fact of different individuals being in such close proximity may afford some protection from enemies both as regards the egg and the offspring, and in so far as there is a mutual advantage such assemblages may be spoken of as communities. A community, however, in the true sense of the word, is a collection of individuals brought together, not primarily as a result of shortage of breeding ground, but in consequence of advantages of communal ownership over individual ownership. A rookery is an example of a true community. Neither shortage of nesting accommodation nor scarcity of food can account for Rooks assembling together to breed; for if the different pairs which go to make up the rookery were to scatter throughout the surrounding neighbourhood, they would, as a rule, find plenty of trees in which to build their nests, and plenty of food.

How, then, can the theory apply to a species that breeds under such conditions? What part can the territory play in furthering the life of the individual when large numbers of nests are built closely together in the same tree? There is much evidence to show that mutual protection is a necessary condition of the Rook's existence; many cases are on record of rookeries being destroyed by Carrion-Crows, Hooded Crows, and Ravens. For instance, Mr. Ward Fowler records a case in which a pair of Crows attacked a small rookery, ransacked the nests, 203 and destroyed the eggs, with the result that not a single pair of Rooks was left in the settlement. Each Rook must therefore secure a position within the precincts of the community if it is to have a chance of success in the attainment of reproduction. But every locality cannot supply sufficient trees of the right kind, appropriately situated and in suitable relation to the food supply, in which numbers of nests can be built in close proximity; so that if more than one community were to attempt to establish itself in a limited area, the supply of food or the supply of trees might become a pressing problem. Each community must therefore be prepared to defend its own interests, and each must be regarded as one unit and the area occupied as one territory within which are included a number of lesser territories. The individual may fail to establish itself within a community, but, even if it succeeds, the community may fail to establish the rights of communal ownership; hence it has to face a twofold possibility of failure, and if it lacked the inherited nature which leads the Guillemot to secure a position upon the ledge, or the Bunting to obtain a position in the marsh, the chances are that it would fail in the attainment of reproduction.

The question now arises as to how it comes about that the area occupied by each individual conforms in broad outline to that which has proved beneficial for the welfare of the species as a whole. We shall find that up to a point the answer is a simple one. No one could study 204 the behaviour of animals without observing the important part that habit plays in the life of the individual; an action performed to-day is liable to be repeated to-morrow and the following day until it becomes ingrained in the life of the individual. This must not be taken to mean, however, that a particular action has to be performed for many days in succession before it becomes definitely fixed; if only it is repeated a number of times, even within the space of a few hours, it will acquire sufficient strength for its continuance; but continued repetition gives increased fixity, and, as time goes by, it becomes increasingly difficult for the creature to make a change unless the character of the situation necessitates readjustment.

For example, when the organic condition which leads to nest-building becomes active, the bird tentatively collects some of the necessary material in its bill, flies round with it, and then drops it. After a while it collects some more, and this time leaves it perhaps in a bush. Later on it makes another attempt, and, meeting with a situation which calls forth the appropriate response, it thereupon lays the foundation of the structure. We will assume that the nest is placed in the midst of a tangled bush. Well, the bird lays the first strands of the foundation and then goes in search of more material. The next time it approaches the nest from the opposite side of the bush, and presently it finds yet a third entrance. But each entrance is not made use of in turn: one is employed 205 more frequently than the other two, and in the course of time becomes the sole highway to and from the nest. Suppose now that, when the young are hatched, I cut away the foliage from the bush on the opposite side from that on which the bird customarily enters, and by so doing leave the nest exposed, what is the result? The female arrives with food, threads her way through the bush, and, when beside the nest, pauses as if aware that some change had taken place, and then flies away through the new opening. In a short time she returns, flits from twig to twig on the outskirts of the bush, and comes upon the new opening—there she hesitates. But though the nest is in full view and within a few inches of her perch, and though the young stretch out their necks, yet so strong is the former habit that she is compelled to return to the opposite side and approach the nest by the usual circuitous route before she distributes the food amongst her offspring.

Let us see how far this law of habit formation may have been effective in defining the extent of the area occupied. When a male Warbler arrives at its destination in the spring it seeks out a suitable environment, and, having found a place unoccupied by any other male, settles in it and remains there—its behaviour up to this point being determined by racial preparation. After the fatigue of the journey its movements are at first sluggish; hunger, however, asserts itself and a search is made for food; wandering away from the position in 206 which it first settled and which acts as a headquarters, it hunts through certain trees here or certain bushes there and returns, and presently it wanders away again, perhaps in another direction, but, as before, works its way back again to the headquarters. The journeys thus radiate outwards from the headquarters, and according to the success with which the bird meets, so, probably, it happens that some trees are searched more often than others and certain directions are taken more frequently than others, and by constant repetition a routine is established which limits the direction and scope of its wanderings.

But in the case of the Guillemot the conditions of existence are reversed: food can be had in abundance but suitable breeding stations are scarce. The few square feet of ledge correspond to the tree or clump of bushes which acts as a headquarters for the Warbler, and the occupation of them is determined, as it is in the case of the Warbler, by racial preparation. Since, however, the ledge is only made use of for the immediate purpose of incubation and is in no way affected by questions relating to food, there is no occasion for the bird to wander along the ledge nor to encroach upon those adjoining. Hunger stimulates the Warbler to search the surrounding trees, and so to extend its area; but hunger takes the Guillemot down to the water, and hence the area which it primarily occupied remains unmodified.

207 To sum up: the territory is useful in various ways, but not necessarily in the same way for every species. Reproduction would always have remained fortuitous, and the number of individuals that attained to it would seldom have reached the possible maximum unless some provision had been included in its system for insuring that the males and females could meet at the proper moment and afterwards remain in touch with one another, and that the number of pairs inhabiting a given area did not exceed the available means of support. I have tried to show that the inclusion of a disposition to secure a territory tends to remove these difficulties. In the first place, the disposition which leads to its occupation comes into functional activity (in the male) early in the season; and so, by the time that the appropriate pairing condition arises in the females, the process of acquiring territories is well advanced, and the males being regularly distributed, each in its respective position, are readily found by their prospective mates. The behaviour of each sex is thus adjusted to further the end of mutual discovery. Next, after mating has taken place, the position occupied by the male acts as a headquarters to which the birds can always repair, and becomes a bond of union which is serviceable in that it prevents any possibility of their drifting apart. And in the third place, the males become pugnacious and in this way secure for themselves areas which vary in size according to the conditions of existence of the species, so that 208 there is no possibility of too many congregating in this locality, and all the less likelihood of too few finding their way to that; and hence, on the average, different pairs are distributed throughout all suitable localities. Furthermore, ow-

ing to the fact of their having a headquarters, the male and female are allowed a freedom of movement which otherwise they would only possess when the construction of the nest had actually begun; they can seek their food independently, and, even though paired, they can if necessary continue their winter routine without risk of separation. This means that the organic condition which leads to pairing, is free to develop in the female earlier than would be the case if there were nothing in the external environment to attract the pair to a particular spot; and the longer the period over which the process of pairing can be spread, the greater chance will females have of discovering mates, the less severe will the competition tend to become, and, consequently, the smaller the percentage of individuals that fail to obtain suitable partners.

In these ways the territory has been serviceable alike to a number of species. But much as the questions of mutual discovery and regular distribution may have influenced the course of its development, there can, I think, be little doubt that, on the one hand, the supply of the necessary accommodation for rearing offspring, and on the other, the necessity for an adequate supply of food in close proximity to the nest, have been the main determining factors, and have led to a wide divergence in its function. At the one extreme the function is to insure a plentiful supply of food for the young; at the other, to insure a station suitable for rearing offspring. I took the Bunting and the Guillemot as types of the two extremes. The young of the former species are born in a very helpless state. They are susceptible to cold and unable to withstand prolonged exposure, and therefore it is essential that there should be an ample supply of food, upon which the parents can draw liberally, in the vicinity of the nest. But the nest is placed in a variety of situations, and accommodation in this respect may be said to be unlimited. The young of the latter species are not so susceptible to exposure, and moreover there is always an abundance of food in the waters beneath the cliff; but ledges of rock, upon which the egg can be securely deposited and the young successfully reared, are limited both in number and extent. The position then is as follows: there are situations in plenty in which hosts of Buntings can build their nests but the supply of food is a difficulty, and if the respective areas of different individuals were insufficient to supply them with the necessary food with the necessary rapidity, they would run the risk of losing their offspring and the species would not endure; on the other hand, cliffs upon which the Guillemot can rear its young are limited, but the supply of food presents no difficulty, and consequently the smaller the area over which each individual exercises dominion, the greater the number that will attain to reproduction and the greater prospect the species will have of survival. The emphasis in the one case lies on the fact that the area occupied must be sufficiently large; on the other, on its being just sufficient and no more to accommodate the egg. Hence the difference in the function at the opposite extremes is brought about, not by modifications of the instinctive behaviour which leads to the establishment and defence of the territory, but solely by modifications in the size of the area occupied, in accordance with the conditions prevailing in the external environment. No doubt, if we had the life-histories of a sufficient number of species worked out, we should find that the gradations were complete from the one extreme to the other. We are justified in thinking that this must be so because in many directions we can not only observe differences in the size of the area occupied, but can recognise a close correspondence between those differences and the conditions of life of the species. Thus the Herring-Gull occupies a comparatively small area, though one which is many times larger than that of the Guillemot. It requires more space because it not only builds a nest but rears four instead of a single offspring, and it can be allowed more space because the young remain in the nest until they are capable of sustained flight, and consequently it can make use of many miles of cliff from which the tide recedes at the base, and which on this account are denied to the Guillemot, but manifestly it cannot be allowed so much space as the Bunting, for then comparatively few individuals would attain to reproduction.

Again, the Reed-Warbler inhabits swamps overgrown with the common reed, and in such places insect life is abundant just at the time when the young are hatched. But these swamps cover a comparatively small acreage in the breeding range of the bird, and if each pair were to attempt to establish dominion over an area equal, let us say, to that of the Willow-Warbler, the species would have but a poor chance in the struggle for existence. So that, in a case of this description, the supply of food and the comparative scarcity of breeding stations have been factors of like importance in the evolution of the territory.

Finally we were led to inquire as to how it comes about that the extent of the area occupied by each individual is adapted to the circumstances in which the individual finds itself; and we came to the conclusion that the movements of the bird, subsequent to the initial act of establishing itself in a position, are regulated and defined by the law of habit formation. For example, the Warbler, in response to its inherited nature, takes up a position in an appropriate situation. It then proceeds to search for food; it makes short journeys first in this direction and then in that; it repeats these journeys, and gradually forms a habit which compels it to remain within more or less well-defined boundaries. But the actual distance that it traverses on the occasion of its first attempt must be determined by the relative abundance or scarcity of the particular kind of insect life which it requires. So that, although habit defines and in some measure helps to determine the boundaries of the territory, it is clear that in the last resort they must depend upon the nature of the conditions in the external environment.

We have, then, the congenital basis which leads to the occupation of a position, and to the enmity shown by the owner of the position towards other individuals; and this congenital basis is found alike in many widely divergent forms, living under equally widely divergent conditions; we have acquired accommodation; and we have relationships in the organic and inorganic world—and the outcome of it all is a system of behaviour which we, who can perceive the end to which such behaviour is tending, are justified in speaking of as "a disposition to secure a territory. " In the development of this system a primary value must be ascribed to the conditions in the external environment, for they determine the direction of the variations of instinctive procedure and of acquired habit which work towards the same goal—that of adjustment to the conditions of life.

NOTE

The following are the experiments referred to on page 181:—

On the 14th May 1915, a nest of Blackbirds approximately four days old was removed at 6.45 A.M. The temperature was considerably below the normal, and snow lay on all the high ground in the neighbourhood. In a short time the birds collapsed, and at 9.15 A. M. were dead. On the 29th May, at 6 A. M. , a second nest was removed, containing young of approximately the same age, and although the conditions were more normal, the temperature being 50° F., the birds collapsed at 8 A. M. , and an hour later one of the brood showed little signs of life. The wind, however, then changed to the west, and the temperature rose one degree, with the result that they were still living at 11 A.M . A further experiment was made with Song-Thrushes on the 5th June. The wind was in the south and the temperature 63° F. The young, approximately four days old, were removed at 7.25 A.M. , but as they showed no signs of collapse at 1 P.M. I replaced the nest in the original site.

On the 30th May, a nest of Whitethroats three days old was removed at 7.15 A.M. The wind was northerly and the weather fine, but the temperature low—50° F. At 8.15 A.M. the birds showed no sign of life. A second experiment with this species was made on the 10th June under more favourable circumstances, for although the sky was overcast and the wind northerly, the temperature was 59° F. In this case the young survived from 6.55 A.M. to 7 P.M.

On the 27th May 1915, a nest of Hedge-Sparrows hatched the previous day was removed at 7 A.M. The temperature was below the normal, being 49° F. At 214 8 A.M. the young were cold and in a state of collapse, but they survived nevertheless until 3.20 P.M.

On the 7th June 1915, a nest of young Skylarks three days old was removed at 7.15 A.M. The temperature was 62° F., and the birds survived until 4 A.M. the next day.

On the 6th June 1916, a nest of Linnets just hatched was removed at 6.47 A.M. The temperature was 51° F. At 7. 50 A M. the birds were cold and in a state of collapse, and only survived until 8.50 A.M.

CHAPTER VI

THE WARFARE BETWEEN DIFFERENT SPECIES AND ITS RELATION TO THE TERRITORY

We have now considered the various ways in which the territory is useful in furthering the life of the individual. We have seen that, in some cases, there is competition for stations where the egg or eggs can be deposited and incubated in safety; that, in others, there is competition for stations capable of furnishing an adequate supply of food for the young; and that the establishment of "territories" not only renders the attainment of reproduction for the individual secure, but serves so to regulate the distribution of pairs that the maximum number can be accommodated in the minimum area. This being so, the question arises as to whether competition for territory is strictly limited to individuals of the same species, or whether it may not occur also between different kinds of birds, providing always that similar conditions of existence are required. First of all I shall relate a number of facts which will serve to show the nature and extent of the warfare, and I shall then give the reasons which lead me to believe that the fighting not only bears some relation to the "territory." but that it is an important factor in contributing to the attainment of that which for biological interpretation is the end for which the whole territorial system has been evolved.

Those who have studied wild life or one of the rocky headlands, which are so numerous round our coasts, will probably be familiar with the rivalry that exists between the Raven and certain birds of prey. Where the Raven finds shelter for its nest, there, too, the Peregrine has its eyrie—and so it happens that these two species are continually at war. Now the warfare occurs not only during the season of reproduction but continues throughout the greater part of the year, and can even be observed in the late summer or early autumn—the period when we should expect to find the instinct least susceptible to appropriate stimulation. But it is of a more determined kind early in the spring, and it is then that we often witness those remarkable exhibitions of flight, the skill of which excites our admiration. The Falcon rises above the Raven, stoops at it, and when it seems no longer possible for a collision to be avoided, or, one would imagine, for the Raven to escape destruction, the Raven skilfully turns upon its back and momentarily faces its opponent, and the Falcon with equal skill changes its course, passing upwards and away. The attack, however, is soon repeated, and though no collision may actually take place, yet the fact that the Raven, when it turns to face its adversary, is obliged to drop the stick which it carries, is not only an indication of the character of the struggle, but it shows that a definite end is gained—that the efforts of the Raven to build in that particular locality are hampered. But the Falcon is not the only enemy that the Raven has to face; Buzzards are just as intolerant of the presence of Ravens in their neighbourhood as the Ravens are of them, and consequently there is incessant quarrelling wherever the same locality is inhabited. As a rule, the fighting occurs whilst the birds are on the wing; the Buzzard rises to a considerable height, and, closing its wings, stoops at the Raven below, and when within a short distance of its adversary, swerves upwards and gains a position from which it can again attack. The Buzzard, however, is by no means always the aggressor; I have watched one so persistently harassed by a Raven that at length it left the rock upon which it was resting and disappeared from view, still followed by its rival. Thus it seems as if they were evenly matched, and, when they occupy the same locality, it is interesting to notice how the initiative passes from the one to the other according to the position occupied by the birds in their respective territories.

Peregrine Falcon attacking a Raven

That there is constant warfare between the Green Woodpecker and the Starling is well known, the purpose of the Starling being to 218 gain possession of the hole which the Woodpecker with much skill has drilled for itself. As far as my experience goes, the Starling is always the aggressor, and there is only too good reason to fear that, in the course of time, the Green Woodpecker will disappear as a result of the greater fertility and tenacity of its enemy. The Martin suffers a similar kind of persecution from the House-Sparrow, and here again there is reason to believe that the greater virility of the Sparrow will hasten the extinction of its rival. In cases of this description the purpose of the fighting is clear, and one can understand why such divergent species should be hostile to one another; yet others, equally remote in the scale of nature, are hostile when no such ostensible reason can be assigned for their hostility. Few birds are more pugnacious than the Moor-Hen, and the determined manner in which different individuals fight with one another is notorious. But the intolerance it displays towards other species is no less remarkable, and its pugnacious instinct seems to be peculiarly susceptible to stimulation by different individuals belonging to widely divergent forms. At one moment a Lapwing may be attacked, at another a Thrush or a Starling, harmless strangers that have approached the pool to drink; even a Water-Rail, as it threads its way through the rushes, may fail to escape detection; and, which is still more curious, a covey of Partridges will evoke response if they approach the pool too closely.

219 Here is a curious instance of apparent waste of energy. A pair of Magpies built their nest in an ilex tree. Early one morning there was a commotion in the tree, much flapping of wings and a medley of sounds which told of large birds engaged in a struggle—the Magpies were attacking a pair of Wood-Pigeons. There was no question as to the genuineness of the struggle, nor any doubt as to the proximate end for which the Magpies were striving, for their efforts continued so long as the Wood-Pigeons remained in the tree, and only ceased when they had succeeded in driving them away.

Turning next to species which are less distantly related, we find that instances of intolerance are more numerous and that a wider range of species is involved. The hostility that the Lapwing displays towards the Snipe calls for special remark. It often happens that the marshes or water meadows, that are such favourite haunts of the Lapwing, are also resorted to by Snipe for the purpose of securing food, or it may be even for the purpose of reproduction. In such places both species are often abundant; the meadow is divided up into Lapwings' territories, and early in the season the Snipe wander over it in small parties, singly, or in pairs. Now, if it were only on isolated occasions that the Lapwing paid heed to the Snipe, one would not perhaps attach any peculiar significance to the fact; but the pugnacious instinct of the bird responds to the presence of this intruder almost as freely as it 220 does to that of another Lapwing. Again and again, day after day, the Snipe are attacked and driven off in a manner which would be fittingly described as persistent persecution, for the Snipe has neither the physical capacity nor apparently any instinctive tendency to retaliate. Thus a Lapwing may come suddenly upon a small party of Snipe hidden from view in a dyke where they are probing the ground for food; the Snipe immediately rise and fly away and there is momentary confusion as the Lapwing darts first at this one, then at that; or, espying a Snipe at rest at the opposite end of its territory, it will first of all run rapidly towards it, and then fly after it, as, with twisting flight, it darts hither and thither a few feet above the ground; or again, it will attack and rapidly pursue solitary individuals as they skim across its territory and attempt to settle. Is this intolerance merely an exuberant expression of an instinct which is serviceable in another direction? The behaviour of the Lapwing scarcely justifies such a conclusion, for all its actions denote a striving towards some end which we can describe, and it seems to gain satisfaction only when the ejection of the intruder has been accomplished.

Many of the Warblers display irritation when approached by other birds which we should scarcely expect would arouse their hostility. The Hedge-Sparrow, for example, is frequently regarded with suspicion, and it is by no means unusual to see it attacked by so 221 small a bird as the Chiffchaff. The Wood-Warbler is also pugnacious, and will even attack a pair of Chaffinches. Between the Tit family and some of the smaller Warblers there are constant exhibitions of hostility; even the Great Tit is liable to be driven away, but the Blue Tit is especially marked out for persecution, though doubtless it is well able to hold its own.

The following incident will show

how real is the antagonism between these two families. A Chiffchaff occupied the corner of a small osier bed, and was particularly aggressive towards other closely-related forms in its immediate neighbourhood. On two mornings in succession ten Blue Tits invaded its ground, passing from end to end of it as they wended their way from tree to tree in search of food. Their presence evoked the usual hostile response, yet, withal, aroused the fear of the Chiffchaff, which, at times, appeared to be swayed by conflicting impulses. Now, in attempting to interpret the nature of the instinct which was evoked, one has to be guided, in a case of this description, by the similarity of the response to that which can be observed on other occasions and in other situations when the intention of the bird is clear. And on this occasion the Chiffchaff betrayed all the symptoms which normally precede an attack; it spread its tail, quivered its wings, uttered its high-pitched note rapidly, hopped from twig to twig, or flew restlessly from tree to tree, and seemed to be prevented from attacking only by the number 222 of its opponents. This, indeed, was shown by its subsequent behaviour, for whenever a Tit became temporarily detached from its companions it hesitated no longer but forthwith attacked.

There are other species which are no less aggressive than the Warblers—the Chats for example. The Stonechat regards with suspicion almost any bird of its own size, and will even pursue a Tree-Pipit if it approaches too closely. The same is true of the Whinchat, and one would scarcely expect to find this bird attacking Buntings as it sometimes does. A Whinchat that occupied some marshy ground was constantly at war with a pair of Reed-Buntings; their territories were adjacent and in some measure overlapped, and the Whinchat drove away either sex indiscriminately, and was not only always the aggressor but seemed to be master of the situation.

Coming now to kindred forms, those, that is to say, which belong to the same family, we find that, both in intensity and extent, the warfare far exceeds anything that we have thus far considered. So frequent, indeed, are acts of intolerance, and so readily awakened into activity is the pugnacious nature of the bird, that the fighting will almost bear comparison in volume with that which occurs between individuals of the same species. Between the Thrush and the Blackbird there are incessant quarrels early in the year, and the initiative seems to pass from one to the other according to 223 the circumstances in which they are placed. If the territory of a Thrush is invaded the Thrush is the aggressor, and, conversely, if that of the Blackbird is threatened, the Blackbird becomes the aggressor; and so, when the territories of the two birds are adjacent or overlap, as frequently they do, there is constant friction, resulting in quarrels which attract attention on account of the noisiness of the birds.

All the Warblers are exceedingly pugnacious, the fighting being especially severe between those that are very closely related. The Blackcap and the Garden-Warbler are constant rivals, and the scenes which can be witnessed when the two meet in competition are interesting from many points of view. The birds not only pursue and fight with one another, but their emotional behaviour reaches a high level of intensity—excitable outbursts of song are indulged in, tails are outspread, wings are slowly flapped, and feathers raised—in fact the attitudes assumed are similar in all respects to those which occur during the contests which are so frequent between the respective individuals of each species; and it would be difficult to point to any one item of behaviour which is not also manifest at one time or another during the battles between these rivals, and still more difficult to trace any difference in the intensity of the excitement. And if we are satisfied that the fighting in the one case is purposive, so, too, must we regard it as having some biological purpose to serve in the other. But the Garden-Warbler 224 is not the only bird that acts as a stimulus to the instinct of the Blackcap; Whitethroats are often attacked, and the Chiffchaff is a source of irritation. Even when a male Blackcap is engaged in incubation, it will leave its nest on the approach of a Chiffchaff, and, having driven away the intruder, proceed to sing excitedly. At other times both male and female will combine to attack this small intruder.

But this does not mean that the Chiffchaff suffers persecution; it is itself most aggressive, as is shown by the fact that it will join in the Blackcap quarrels and attack the combatants indiscriminately. Its behaviour, however, requires further consideration, especially as regards its relations with its nearest of kin—the Willow-Warbler; for here we have a mutual intolerance which is somewhat remarkable, and evidence of it can be found wherever the birds occupy the same ground. Now it can be observed that the hostility is not limited merely to occasional acts of intolerance, but that there is organised warfare lasting, it may be, for many days in succession, and that the actions of the birds bear the stamp of a persistent striving towards some end. On one occasion the Willow-Warbler may be the aggressor, on another the Chiffchaff, and at times it is difficult to say which of the two is responsible for the quarrel. In size and in strength they are equal, and the "will to fight" is as strong in the one as in the other, so that it is seldom, if ever, possible to point to 225 this one as the victor and that one as the vanquished. Success or failure probably depends more upon the cumulative effect of many combats entailing physical exhaustion, than upon the issue of any one particular battle; and whilst observation might quite well fail to distinguish any resultant change in the relative positions of the birds, or any harmful effect upon their constitutions, yet the area occupied by this one might be sufficiently curtailed to prejudice the welfare of the young, or the vitality of that one might be seriously impaired—and we should be none the wiser.

Neither the Marsh-Warbler nor the Reed-Warbler will tolerate strangers within the small space of ground over which they exercise dominion. Of the two, the Marsh-Warbler is perhaps the more pugnacious, and will attack any other Warbler that approaches too closely; Whitethroats are often pursued and driven away, and less frequently, Garden-Warblers. In one case, a male occupied the same ground as a Sedge-Warbler, and there was a constant feud between them; a willow-tree formed its headquarters, and this same tree seemed to be the headquarters of the Sedge-Warbler, so that they often met and whenever they did so they quarrelled. As a rule the Marsh-Warbler was the aggressor and had the mastery over its opponent, and when it attacked, it uttered a peculiar harsh scolding note, raised the feathers on its back, spread out its wings, and betrayed the usual symptoms of emotional excitement.

226 On the other hand, the Sedge-Warbler is most aggressive towards other kindred species, and when a male happens to occupy the same ground as a Reed-Warbler, there are frequent battles between them and incessant commotion; they fly at one another and meet in the air with an audible clicking of bills, or pursue one another amongst the reeds, each one uttering its characteristic scolding note.

The Tits, as a family, are notoriously pugnacious. I have seen a pair of Blue Tits attack a single Long-tailed Tit with great determination, and not only did they pursue it, but, flying at it, struck it with considerable force.

In giving an account of the domestic economy of the Carrion-Crow, Mr. Edmund Selous refers to the hostility between this bird and the Magpie. "About a week ago," he says, 6 "I saw a Crow busily engaged in chasing away several Magpies, not only from three or four tall slender trees close together, in one of which it had its nest, but also from various other trees, not far off, round about. In this the Crow had a good deal of trouble, as the Magpies were always returning. After a time it was joined by another crow, which however did not take so active a part in the drama, nor did I see either of the two actually go to the nest, though I could only explain their action by supposing it was their own. This morning I saw the same thing reversed, for a pair of 227 Magpies, with an undoubted nest, kept attacking a Crow that insisted on settling in one of a row of trees—also tall and slender—in which it was placed. Both were equally persevering—the Crow, though often chased away, always returning, and settling generally in the last tree of the row, where he would be left alone sometimes for a minute or two, but before long one of the Magpies flew at him, and put him to flight. The Crow defended itself, but not, it would seem, very successfully, and in the last attack upon him, made, with great spirit, in the air, a large black feather floated to the ground, which I made no doubt was his. Yet this did not drive him from the trees, and it was only on my approaching nearer that he finally left them. Thus we see that both species look upon the approach of the other to within a moderate distance of their nest as an intrusion."

That the Rook suffers persecution from the Carrion-Crow is a well-established fact, and there is reason to believe that it has another dangerous enemy in the Hooded Crow. According to the late Mr. Ussher, Choughs will attack both Hooded Crows and Ravens. "I once saw," he says, "two Choughs energetically attacking a pair of Ravens; they shot up into the air and darted down on the latter, whose heavy flight made them helpless against their agile tormentors."

Birds of prey are often hostile to one another. The Merlin is exceptionally pugnacious, and its boldness in attacking intruders is well known. 228 When, for example, a Kestrel approaches its territory, it leaves the tree, bush, or rock upon which it was resting, utters its characteristic cry, and soars rapidly upwards; then, rising to a considerable height, it swoops down upon the Kestrel, and by alternately stooping at and chasing its opponent, drives it away from the immediate neighbourhood.

What we have, then, to consider is, Do these battles between different species contribute towards the attainment of the end for which the whole territorial system has been evolved?

Let us take the individual and see whether we can establish any relation between the hostility it displays towards members of other species and its general disposition to secure a territory. We must remember that a male can have no knowledge of the prospective value of its behaviour, nor is it likely that it has any ulterior purpose in ejecting other males, beyond the pleasure it derives from satisfying its impulse to do so. The proximate end of its behaviour is to attack, nothing more, and this, of course, it can only do just in so far as the intruder evokes the appropriate instinct.

Now the arguments we shall employ will, on the whole, be similar to those which we made use of in the second chapter, wherein we attempted to ascertain the conditions under which a male becomes intolerant of other males of its own species, and examined more especially the claims of the "territory" as opposed to those of the "female." But here 229 we start on firmer ground, because the one factor which introduced an element of uncertainty—the female—can be definitely excluded; at least it seems so to me, for granting even that her presence is the condition under which the pugnacious nature of the male is rendered susceptible to stimulation, it is difficult to see why a male of a different species should supply that stimulus, or what biological purpose could be served by its doing so.

When dealing with the attitude of a male towards others of its kind, we attached considerable significance to the fact that its pugnacious nature gained or lost susceptibility according to the position which it happened to occupy. We found, it will be remembered, that the same bird that was pugnacious in its own territory took no further interest in its opponent when the boundary was passed; and, moreover, that if it happened to wander into an adjoining one, it made no real effort to defend itself when attacked, but returned forthwith to its own headquarters. It remains to be shown whether the rivalry between different kinds of birds is similarly related to the position which the opponents happen to occupy at the time.

First, then, there is the general consideration, namely, that the enmity occurs for the most part just at the time when the territories are in process of being established. During autumn and winter, many birds of more or less close affinity assemble together in flocks, wherever the supply of food is abundant, and are then 230 not only sociable, but, so there is reason to believe, are mutually helpful both in discovering the necessary means of subsistence which are often none too plentiful, and in affording protection from enemies, which, on the contrary, are often numerous. That the different units of which these flocks are composed should live on amicable terms is therefore as necessary for the welfare of the whole community at this particular season as that the different individuals of the same species should do so. But just as the sociable relations, which obtain between these individuals throughout the winter, undergo a marked change at the commencement of the breeding season, so, too, do different species, which habitually associate together, suddenly become hostile to one another. This change is coincident in time with the rise of the organic condition which leads to the establishment of territories; and the hostility continues, though in diminishing degree, throughout the breeding season, and dies away the following autumn.

For example, different Warblers resort to the elders (*Sambucus nigra*) in September, and there pass much time feeding on the fruit which is then ripe and often abundant. In the same bush there may be Blackcaps, Garden-Warblers, Whitethroats, and Lesser Whitethroats, some preening their feathers, others searching for the berries, others again, with feathers relaxed, making feeble attempts to sing. Occasionally there may be a scuffle, perhaps between a 231 Blackcap and a Lesser Whitethroat, or between a Garden-Warbler and a Blackcap, but it is of short duration and lacks vigour. Apart, however, from such temporary disturbances, there is no real rupture in their relations, and certainly nothing to lead one to suppose that the bickerings are determined by the functioning of any specific instinct. Yet only a few months previously some of them were constantly at war, and their quarrels betrayed symptoms of great persistence; and if we remember how the observed behaviour of the birds suggests the fact that they were striving to attain something definite, we shall understand the nature and extent of the change, and shall, I fancy, be in a better position to estimate its biological worth at its true value.

We can find many similar examples—flocks are to be found on arable ground, on the water meadows, and on the mud-flats; here different kinds of Thrushes feed on the berries of the yew, there different kinds of Tits travel together in parties; hosts of Finches collect in the hollies to pass the night and Buntings roost together in the gorse; and, in fact, in whatever direction we choose to look in the autumn and winter, we find various birds assembled together and living on amicable terms. All of this changes in the spring, and the relationship undergoes a gradual but noticeable alteration; so much so that whereas the outstanding feature of bird life in the winter is sociability, that of the spring is hostility. 232

So much, then, for the seasonal change of relationship; let us now turn to particular cases and attempt to trace the condition which accompanies such change.

Many migrants in the spring seem to follow the course of the Severn during their journey northwards through Worcestershire; and where the river bends to the north-west at Lincombe Lock, there they leave it, or, rather, continue in a north-easterly direction which takes them across the southern end of Hartlebury Common. As I have already mentioned, this Common is overgrown with gorse, heather, and ling, and scattered here and there are a number of dwarf oak-trees and small elder-bushes. The situation is therefore an ideal one for the smaller migrants to rest for a brief time, and, from the point of view of the observer, very suitable because it is open and the movements of the birds can be traced for some distance. Turtle Doves pass over at a great height, or skim across a few feet above the gorse; Redstarts settle for a few minutes and then disappear; Tree-Pipits, Whinchats, and Willow-Warblers pass from tree to tree or flit from bush to bush—and all in a north-easterly direction. They do not sing, they are restless, and, judging by their behaviour, they are anxious to conceal their presence, not to make it known. Yet we know that when they reach their destination, as presently they will, all this will change; that each of them will employ every means at its disposal to make itself conspicuous; and that 233 each, as far as it is able, will resist intrusion on the part of other species.

Now the southern end of the Common is always inhabited by individuals belonging to one of these species, or to others of close affinity; so that wherever these travellers settle whilst passing across it, the chances are that they will find the ground occupied—and their behaviour under such circumstances is no less interesting than the behaviour of the bird upon whose ground they are trespassing. We will take the case of the Whinchat. It arrives from the southwest, and, flying from bush to bush, works its way in a north-easterly direction. In doing so it intrudes upon the territory of a Stonechat; and the Stonechat, becoming excited, flies towards it, and it retires for a short distance in the direction from whence it came. Here again it is followed and attacked and again moves on, and then, flying in a circle as if to avoid the territory which blocked the path, resumes its former line of flight, though still followed by the Stonechat, which after continuing the pursuit for perhaps a quarter of a mile, suddenly turns in the air and returns to its headquarters.

It is difficult to put oneself in the place of the Stonechat or of the Whinchat. But even after making due allowance for the danger inseparable from any attempt to do so, there remains the unquestionable fact that whereas the impulse to attack was strong in the one, the impulse to defend itself was wholly lacking in 234 the other. Yet a Whinchat, when it has established itself, is most pugnacious; it not only attacks every bird of a similar size that approaches its position, but its behaviour under such circumstances bears the impress of unusual determination; and if we were to take a male and place it in the position of the Stonechat, we should find that its nature would change, that the presence of the Stonechat would evoke a hostile response, and, conversely, that the instinct of the Stonechat would not be susceptible to stimulation. Hence it is clear that the nature of a bird when on migration is not quite the same as it is when its destination is reached; that the positions occupied from time to time during the journey carry no meaning, or, rather, are not brought into relation with its life in quite the same way as is the position which it finally occupies; and further, it is clear that the interest it displays in other species undergoes a somewhat remarkable transformation when at length its destination is reached.

This altered nature of the migrant is a fact of some importance in relation to our present subject, but it does not stand alone—the same characteristic is observable in other phases of bird life. Some of the residents, the Buntings and the Finches for example, occupy their breeding ground very early in the year, and it often happens that the situations which they select are not capable of supplying them with food so early in the season, though at a later date food will be there in abundance; so that 235 they are compelled to resort to the surrounding neighbourhood, and since, even there, the available supply is sometimes scarce or, if plentiful, limited to certain areas, they are constrained from time to time to join together again in flocks. Thus, for part of the year, they may be said to lead a double existence; for just as the Whinchat, that is sociable on migration, betrays a changed nature when it reaches its destination, so too does the nature of these residents change from hour to hour according to whether they are seeking food or occupying the breeding ground.

In the newly-sown fields of grain the birds frequently find a supply of food. Here Yellow Buntings, Greenfinches, and Chaffinches collect from the surrounding neighbourhood. The majority are somewhere in possession of territories, and not a few are paired. Between the territories and the feeding ground a highway is formed by individuals passing to and fro. Sometimes both members of the pair leave together in order to seek food, at other times they separate and the male may be in his territory whilst the female is with the flock. Apart from occasional manifestations of sexual emotion on the part of a male, there is nothing to disturb the harmony of the flock nor anything in the behaviour of the birds which would lead one to suspect that, when they return, their nature will change and that they will be no longer sociable; and, which is still more remarkable, no matter how great the provocation which 236 an individual, when in company with the flock, may be called upon to endure, its customary hostile response will fail to be elicited. An incident which happened in the spring of 1917 will serve to make this clear. A flock of some thirty Yellow Buntings, Greenfinches, and Chaffinches were feeding in one corner of a field which had recently been sown with barley. As they sought their food they wandered outwards into the middle of the field, and in so doing, passed across the territory of a Skylark. Whereupon the Skylark became excited, uttered its call-note rapidly, and rising a few feet from the ground, attacked those members of the flock that were nearest, which happened to be the Yellow Buntings; and so determined were its onslaughts that the Yellow Buntings were forced to retire. The Skylark showed no discrimination as to sex, but attacked both males and females, and within a few minutes succeeded in driving away at least two pairs. One would have expected that the Yellow Buntings would have made some show of resistance; one would have thought that the fact of being violently attacked would have supplied a stimulus sufficiently strong to evoke a corresponding hostile response: yet there was no mistaking the lack of interest that they displayed in the contest—they made no effort to retaliate but seemed to accept the situation as unalterable and left.

So far we have examined only those cases in which the pugnacious instinct was stimulated in 237 one of the adversaries, and in which consequently the fighting seldom reached any high degree of severity. We must now consider some others in which each of the opponents acts as a stimulus to the pugnacious instinct of the other. It is here, of course, that we find the most violently contested battles, and it is here, too, that the purpose of the fighting seems clear. The persecution which the Green Woodpecker suffers from the Starling is well known. The purpose of the Starling's behaviour is clear, namely the possession of the hole occupied by the Woodpecker. Bird for bird, the Woodpecker is more than the equal of the Starling, but persistent endeavour ultimately wins the day. The Starlings perch close beside the hole, and, whenever the Woodpecker shows itself, attack with determination; and not only do they do so but they are assisted, so there is reason to believe, by other individuals or pairs in the attainment of their end, so that no matter how stoutly the Woodpecker defends itself, in time it is almost certain to be deprived of its ownership.

In like manner different kinds of Woodpeckers contend with one another for the possession of a hole, and here the opponents are more equally matched. I have seen a pair of Lesser Spotted Woodpeckers endeavouring to drive away a Great Spotted Woodpecker. The excitement of all three birds was exceptional. Each of the Lesser Spotted Woodpeckers kept swooping in turn at their rival, sometimes in the 238 air and sometimes when it was settled on the topmost branches of a dead tree, and the sounds produced reminded one of the piping of a flock of Oyster-Catchers in flight.

A battle between a pair of Green Woodpeckers and a Great Spotted Woodpecker is worth mentioning. It occurred on the 24th of April. Passing through the middle of a wood, I noticed a Great Spotted Woodpecker fly out of a hole in an oak-tree. Shortly afterwards, a pair of Green Woodpeckers settled near the hole and then flew to some oak-trees close at hand, where they were joined by their rival and signs of hostility were soon apparent. Presently the Great Spotted Woodpecker returned to the hole and entered. Both of the Green Woodpeckers then flew into the tree; and one of them, settling upon the trunk, climbed up to the level of the hole and, when it became aware of the Great Spotted Woodpecker within, extended its wings fully and proceeded to peck viciously at its opponent. Whereupon there was a scuffle at the mouth of the hole and the Great Spotted Woodpecker hurriedly left. After this, all was quiet and the Green Woodpecker eventually descended and entered the hole. The Great Spotted Woodpecker, however, returned again, but, after fluttering around the hole, disappeared, leaving the Green Woodpeckers in possession.

A battle between a pair of Green Woodpeckers and a pair of Pied Woodpeckers for the possession of a hole in an oak tree.

ERRATUM
For "pair of Pied Woodpeckers"
read "Great Spotted Woodpecker"

In this varied field of hostile behaviour which we have explored, one feature stands out prominently, namely, that the interest 239 which a bird displays in other species varies not only at different seasons but even from hour to hour. I have used the word "nature" as equivalent to "interest," and I have spoken of the bird's nature changing or altering according to the circumstances in which it was placed. But its nature is its inborn constitution, and its constitution cannot change from day to day, still less from hour to hour. So that, in a sense, and having regard to strict scientific accuracy, it is misleading in this particular connotation to say that the bird's nature changes.

What then does happen? The instinct of pugnacity must form just as much a part of the hereditary make-up of the migrant, when on migration, as when finally it reaches its destination; still more must it form part of the constitution of the Bunting when it leaves its headquarters temporarily and joins the flock. And, if it is there, the question arises as to why it does not respond. Now every instinct requires for its response a stimulus of an appropriate kind, and, therefore, a reasonable view to take would be that the necessary stimulus was lacking. But this is a view which we cannot uphold because on all these occasions an opposing male was present—and, so far as it is possible to judge by observation, that is the stimulus which in the main evokes a hostile response. We must therefore look elsewhere than in its direction for a reason which will adequately explain the behaviour.

Though it be true that every instinct 240 requires for its functioning a stimulus of an appropriate kind, yet it is also true that the condition which will render it responsive must be present. What we have then to consider is whether the phenomena which we have explored give us any clue as to the particular nature of that condition. In the first place, we have the general fact that the hostility is not confined to a few species belonging to a few families, but that it is of wide application—birds of prey, Warblers, Woodpeckers, all supply us with evidence which serves to show, in greater or less degree, its nature and extent. Next, we found that the hostility was peculiar to a certain season—and that one the season of reproduction. And if the question were asked: What condition would then be most likely to render the instinct susceptible, the answer that would most certainly be given would be—the presence of a female. And in reply to a further question as to the particular nature of the stimulus to which the instinct would respond, we should be told—the presence of another male of the same species. Now the possible influence of the female on the course of the male's behaviour was the subject of inquiry in the second chapter, wherein we endeavoured to explain the hostility between males of the same species, and we came to the conclusion that it was not alone sufficient to account for the facts disclosed. Still less likely, therefore, is it that her presence can bear any direct relation to the hostility 241 between different species, the more so since the biological end of securing a mate is definitely excluded. And we have something in the nature of proof of the correctness of this view in the fact that she accompanies her mate when he joins the flock, and that there his instinct is not susceptible to stimulation. We then proceeded to examine certain cases in which all the indications pointed to the fact that the "will to fight" was present in only one of the opponents; and we attached considerable importance to this circumstance, because we knew from experience that the same bird which seemed to lack courage, could at other times and in other situations be most aggressive. If then we ask what condition was present on the one occasion that was absent on the other, we have no difficulty in finding a reply—on every occasion on which the opponents appeared to be unevenly matched, one was in occupation of a territory and the other was not. And if we inquire further as to which of the two was the aggressor, the answer is again clear, namely, the bird that occupied a territory. Finally we considered some particular instances in which the "will to fight" was present alike in both opponents, and in which the battles were protracted and severe.

But the fact that a bird has established a territory is not in itself sufficient to render its hostile nature susceptible; it must be actually in occupation if a response is to be elicited. We reach this conclusion step by step: the behaviour of the migrant, that lacks the "will to fight" when on migration but is pugnacious when it has secured a territory, shows it; the behaviour of the resident, which temporarily joins the flock and is there sociable, shows it; and it is shown also by the determination with which both opponents fight when the question of ownership of a station is in dispute. And of all the facts we have reviewed, this is perhaps the most important in relation to our present subject, for it demonstrates that the change from sociability to hostility is not merely an incident of the sexual season, not merely an indirect result of the functioning of the general disposition which leads to the establishment of a territory, but that it is intimately associated with the whole process, and that the particular part of the bird's nature which is concerned is so nicely balanced that it will respond under one condition and one only.

Thus we are led to the only conclusion which seems consistent with the facts, namely that there is a relationship between the "territory" and the hostility.

If we are satisfied that all this warfare is not merely an expression of an instinct which is serviceable in another direction, what part does it play in the whole scheme of reproduction?

The young of many birds are delicate at birth and unable to withstand exposure to cold, and in the previous chapter we came to the conclusion that the territory was serviceable in that it provided an adequate supply of food in the vicinity of the nest, and thus obviated the necessity of the parents being absent from them for long. But manifestly no matter how active a male may be in driving away members of its own sex and kind, it will neither make its position secure, nor insure a supply of food for its young, so long as any number of individuals of different kinds are allowed to establish themselves in the same space of ground. On the one hand, then, we have the fact that there is constant strife between males of close affinity, whilst on the other, we know that many species require like conditions of existence and are bound to assemble wherever these conditions are suitable; and we can infer that the territory would fail to serve its purpose if no restriction were imposed upon the measure of such assemblies.

The question then arises: Does all this warfare contribute towards the attainment of reproduction? Not far from my house there is a small water meadow, three acres in extent, which for some years has been derelict and is now overgrown with the common rush (*Juncus communis*) and small alder trees. For three successive seasons I watched the bird life of this meadow, and more especially the Reed-Buntings whose behaviour I was studying at the time. In every respect the meadow was suitable for this bird; there was an abundance of food and numberless situations in which nests could be placed. Each year all the pairs were successful in rearing one, if not two broods, yet the number of pairs never exceeded five—the first year there were three; the second year five; and the third year four. In addition to the four pairs of Reed-Buntings, there were in the spring of 1915, six pairs of Whitethroats, one pair of Lesser Whitethroats, four pairs of Willow-Warblers, one pair of Sedge-Warblers, two pairs of Grasshopper-Warblers, one pair of Chiffchaffs, three pairs of Hedge-Sparrows, two pairs of Tree-Pipits, one pair of Skylarks, one pair of Whinchats, one pair of Flycatchers, two pairs of Song-Thrushes, one pair of Blackbirds, one pair of Redstarts, three pairs of Chaffinches, and one pair of Wrens—in all, thirty-five pairs, whose young were mainly dependent for their living upon the insect life of that meadow and the ground immediately surrounding it. If we allow three young to each pair—and this would take no account of second broods—we arrive at the following result, namely, that one hundred and five young and seventy adults had to be supplied with food from that locality, which would mean, if the search for food were strictly limited to that meadow, that 83 square yards would be allotted to each individual.

Suppose now that the four male Reed-Buntings had each admitted one other male, and that they had secured mates, what would have been the effect upon the whole community? The four additional pairs with their young would have represented twenty individuals, which would have represented a decrease of 8.5 square yards in the space allotted to each individual. The pressure of the bird population upon the means of support would then have been materially increased; and not only the Buntings, but the Warblers, Pipits, and all the rest would have suffered. But the result would have been the same if, instead of the four additional male Reed-Buntings, four males of other kinds had been allowed to enter the marsh, and we can multiply the number four until we arrive at a point when the means of subsistence would no longer have been adequate for the adults, still less for the young. If, then, there were nothing to prevent this happening, many of the birds in that marsh would have no chance of rearing their young successfully. Hence, if the territory is adequately to serve the purpose for which we believe it has been evolved, some provision must have been included in the system to meet the difficulty.

There are three ways by which this may have been accomplished—indirectly, by increasing the size of the area occupied by each individual, and thereby reducing the relative number of each species; or directly, by rendering the fighting instinct of the bird susceptible to stimulation by individuals of other species; or, possibly, by a combination of the two. There were four pairs of Reed-Buntings in the marsh, and their territories covered the whole of it. But inasmuch as other insectivorous birds were established there also, and found sufficient food to maintain both themselves and their families, it is clear that the area these Reed-Buntings occupied was in excess of that which they would have required if they had been the sole inhabitants. And such often appears to be the case. Many a Warbler allocates to itself a space of ground more than sufficient to supply it with all that it needs; so, too, does the Finch, or the Pipit, or the Falcon—if we take no account of kindred species. Thus there is reason to believe that, by limiting the number of individuals in a given locality, this apparently wasteful expanse of territory is serviceable in that it provides against the pressure of the bird population upon the available means of support becoming too great. But though a reduction in the numerical standing of the different species would certainly follow from any increase in the area occupied by the respective individuals, and with even greater certainty would place them in a more secure position as regards their supply of food, yet, when we remember how large a number are dependent upon a supply of insect life for their young, we can understand that it would not alone be a sufficient safeguard against the dangers attendant upon overcrowding. It is here, I believe, that we shall find the true explanation of the hostility; it roughly insures that the number of pairs in any given area does not exceed the available means of support, and indeed it is difficult to imagine how such uniformity of distribution as would free the young from the risk of 247 exposure could be obtained without some such control.

Some birds, however, have no difficulty in finding the necessary food for their young, yet have great difficulty in finding a station where they can rear their young in safety; and the area each one occupies has been reduced to the smallest proportions in order that the maximum number can be accommodated. Here, any increase in the size of the territory would inevitably lead to the extinction of the race, so that nothing stands between failure and success except the ability of the bird to defend its territory. If we study the bird population at one of the breeding stations on the coast, we find, generally speaking, that each kind of bird inhabits a particular portion of the cliff; on the lower ledges are the Guillemots and Kittiwake Gulls; higher up are Razorbills and Fulmars, and at the top, where the cliff is broken and the face of the rock covered with turf and soil, the Puffin finds shelter for its egg. At the same time there is much overlapping; the kind of ledge that suits a Razorbill is equally suitable for a Guillemot or a Fulmar, and so, no matter how successful the Razorbill may be in establishing a territory and preventing intrusion upon it by other Razorbills, it will be all to no purpose if it allows itself to be jostled out of its position by a Fulmar. Hence, inasmuch as breeding stations are limited and competition for territory so severe, only those forms in which the fighting 248 instinct responds freely to a wide range of stimuli will be in a position to maintain a footing upon the cliff.

In trying to estimate the importance of the hostility in its relation to the territory, we must bear in mind that competition varies in different seasons and in different localities. The surface of the land is constantly undergoing modification, partly owing to human and partly to physical agency—forests are cleared; marshes are drained; the face of the sea-cliffs is altered by the erosion of the waves; here the coast may be locally elevated, there locally depressed; and so forth. Many of these changes are slow and imperceptible, many can be observed in our own lifetime. The timber is felled and the undergrowth cleared in some wood, and the following spring we notice a change in the character of the bird population. Migrants which formerly found in it no suitable accommodation now begin to appear, and as the seasons pass by and the undergrowth affords more and more shelter for the nests and an increasing supply of insect life, so their numbers increase until the wood becomes an important breeding station, resonant with the song of many individuals. But slowly the growth increases; the bushes pass into saplings and the saplings into trees, and the undergrowth there disappears just as surely as do the migrants which can no longer find there the conditions which they require.

Or, as an illustration of the effect produced 249 by natural agency, let me describe a change which has taken place in a corner of Co. Donegal. The promontory of Horn Head is bounded on the west by extensive sand-hills, 100 ft. or more in height. On the southern side it is divided from the mainland by a channel, which narrows down to 100 yards or so in width where it fringes the sand-hills and then widens out again, covering an area of approximately 270 acres. As far as is known in the memory of man, this area has always been tidal. But in recent years a change has taken place, and the blown sand has silted up the channel, with the result that this tidal area has been transformed into a brackish lake. What has brought about the change is not easy to determine. There is evidence, however, of a slow alteration of the level of the shore-line; for in the midst of the sand-hills, situated 150 yards or so from the present sea-margin, and running parallel with it, there is an accumulation of pebbles some 3 feet high by 4 feet deep. This raised beach is now separated from the Atlantic by sand-drifts of considerable height, and consequently there are some grounds for believing that secular elevation is taking place, which, if it be the case, will account for the change in progress. Now the effect on the bird population can be seen even now, and will doubtless become more apparent as the years pass by. Sand-Martins used to find plenty of places to breed amongst the sand-drifts, and moreover do so still. But their nesting sites are constantly changing and dis 250 appearing, and the breeding-place of one colony, that was situated in the bank of a stream twelve years ago, is now buried 10 feet or more below the surface of the sand. The area that was once tidal, but is now a brackish lake, is fed by mountain streams, and as the fresh water predominates, so in course of time will it become fringed with vegetation; and instead of the flocks of Curlew, Dunlin, and other waders that, at low water, resorted there to feed, Coots will fight with one another for the possession of territories, and the Wild Duck will teach her young to seek their food.

In whatever direction we turn, we find that many breeding grounds are subject to incessant change. Ancient haunts disappear, new ones come into being, a change which makes life impossible for this bird, as likely as not benefits that one, and so on. There is no stability. Hence in any given district each recurring season there must needs be a large number of individuals which are obliged to seek new stations, and if there were no control over their distribution, if each one were free to establish itself wherever it chanced to alight, this locality might be overcrowded and that one deserted; and, bearing in mind how many species there are that require similar conditions of existence, we can infer that the successful attainment of reproduction would become impossible for many of those individuals so long as each species was indifferent to the presence of the others. On the other hand, if 251 there were no control over the range of the intolerance, the smaller bird would have no chance in competition with the larger, and it is doubtful whether the larger would gain an advantage commensurate with the energy it would expend in ridding its area of the smaller. I have described battles in which the opponents were only distantly related; for instance, the Moor-Hen will attack almost any bird—Partridge, Lapwing, or Starling—that approaches its territory even temporarily. Nevertheless the antagonism between kindred forms is more prevalent, and, as a rule, characterised by more persistent effort; and thus it seems as if the susceptibility of the fighting instinct has its limitations, the degree of the responsiveness being dependent upon the affinity of the opponents.

Suppose now that we take an area inhabited by a number of different species requiring like conditions of existence, divide it into three sections, and imagine that in one they were all sociable, that in another they were all hostile, and that in a third those which were closely related were intolerant of one another. Let us suppose further that each one of them was represented by the full number of individuals that the law of territory would allow. In the first section an individual would establish itself, and, becoming intolerant of its own kind, would exercise dominion over an area roughly sufficient, providing conditions were normal, to insure an adequate supply of food for 252 its young. But it would take no account of other species, and since any number might occupy the same ground, the fact of its having established a territory would not alone suffice to render its supply of food secure. Success in the attainment of reproduction would then become largely a matter of chance, depending upon the number of individuals that happened to settle in this place or in that. In the second section there would be perpetual warfare; for whereas the appropriate organic condition which leads to pairing arises in different species at different times, fresh claimants to occupied ground would constantly be appearing, and the efforts of the inhabitants to preserve their boundaries intact would have to be maintained throughout the whole period of reproduction; and while the stronger or more persistent forms would be more likely to breed, they would do so at the expense of their young, to which they would be unable to devote proper attention, and with an expenditure of energy that would reflect itself upon the future of the race. But the conditions of life in the third section would be such as would be more likely to yield good results. The relations of the different members of the community would be more evenly balanced, for a male would only be called upon to compete with those of its own size and strength. Thus, on the one hand, accommodation would be so divided as to secure the breeding of the maximum number of individuals with the minimum of expenditure of energy, whilst on the other, 253 any undue pressure upon the available means of subsistence would be prevented.

There can be no question that in the latter section a higher percentage of individuals would succeed in rearing offspring. And so, by reason of the fighting instinct being more susceptible or less susceptible according to the affinity of the opponents, a control is established which, while preventing unnecessary extension of warfare, allows for sufficient extension to render the biological end secure.

These, then, are the facts—this the conclusion which can be drawn from them. It may, however, be said of these facts, as it has been said, with even less justification, of the battles between individuals of the same species, that they do not afford evidence of genuine hostility. No doubt there are many naturalists who could supplement these facts with others in which the conflicts resulted in bodily injury, or terminated fatally, or at least were of a more determined kind. But I have already drawn attention to the fact that, so long as a definite result is attained, the severity of the struggle and the amount of injury inflicted are matters of small moment. Let us, however, run over the substance of the argument, and then briefly refer again to this point of view.

After enumerating instances of hostility, sufficient in number, so it seemed, to constitute reasonable ground for the belief that they had a part to play in the life-history of the 254 individual, the two questions we set ourselves to examine in this chapter were: Is there any circumstance in the life behaviour of the individual with which the hostility can be definitely related; and, will the hostility lead to the securing of a greater measure of success in the attainment of reproduction?

Many different species assemble together in winter and roam from place to place in search of food. But in spring their behaviour undergoes a remarkable transformation; they avoid one another and become quarrelsome, so much so that whereas the outstanding feature of the winter is sociability, that of the spring is hostility. With this general fact before us, we proceeded to investigate this change of behaviour still further. First of all we took the case of a migrant, and, comparing its behaviour, as it journeyed, with that when finally it reached its destination, we found that the bird which was notoriously pugnacious when in occupation of a territory betrayed no interest in other species as it travelled to the accustomed breeding ground. Not only so, but even though it was attacked, we found that its pugnacious instinct still failed to respond. Here, however, it may be contended, and with reasonable justification, that in the interval which elapses before the ultimate destination is reached, some change in the organic condition of the bird may occur which will account for its altered behaviour; or, it may be urged, with no less justification, that whereas on 255 migration the bird is unpaired, when the destination is reached it is probably in possession of a mate and is therefore quarrelsome. Now, at the most, the interval can only be a matter of a few days, and it is unlikely that organic changes sufficient to bring about so important an alteration of behaviour could occur in so short a time, still less likely that they could be timed to come into functional activity just at the moment when the bird reaches its breeding ground. And with regard to the suggestion that the change can be accounted for by the presence of a mate, we shall do well to remember not only that males as a rule precede the females by some days, but that a male may even remain in its territory, mateless, for some weeks, and yet display hostility.

Nevertheless the case of the migrant did not, by itself, afford sufficient evidence upon which to base any conclusion. We therefore inquired into the behaviour of some of the residents at a corresponding period. The Bunting served as an illustration. Early in the season it establishes a territory, and because food is then scarce it is forced to seek it elsewhere than on the small plot of ground which it has acquired; and so it makes its way to some spot where the supply is abundant, and there, meeting with other species bent on a similar errand, forms with them a flock. Part of its time is then spent in the territory and part on the feeding ground, and between these two points a 256 highway is formed by the bird passing constantly to and fro. But the attention which it pays to other species is very different on these two occasions—when in the territory it is intolerant of strangers, but when it accompanies the flock it displays no interest in their movements. From hour to hour its nature seems to change. But, as we saw, the inborn constitution of the bird cannot change, and therefore we came to the conclusion that an explanation of the altered behaviour was to be found in the fact that the pugnacious instinct is only rendered susceptible under a certain condition. So that all the evidence tended to confirm the impression which we had gained from the course of events in the life of the migrant, namely, that the hostility bears a direct relation to the occupation of a territory.

Finally we were led to inquire whether the hostility was serviceable in promoting the welfare of the individuals. We saw that many different species require similar conditions of existence, that ancient breeding haunts disappear and that new ones come into being, and that in the ordinary course of events such species must often assemble in the same area for the purpose of reproduction. So that even though a male might be successful in protecting its ground from intruders of its own kind, yet it might still fail to rear offspring, just because it happened to choose a position in which other kindred forms had gathered. Hence if the territory is adequately to serve its purpose, 257 some control over the local distribution of species is of paramount importance. Nevertheless, if all the different forms that require similar conditions of existence were intolerant of one another in a like degree, the smaller bird would have no chance in competition with the larger. This, however, is not the case. Some, as we saw, arouse little or no animosity in others, in fact the more closely related the rivals, the more responsive their pugnacious nature seems to become.

To return now to the view that the fighting is not really serious, but, on the contrary, that it is either vestigial and has no longer any part to play in furthering the life of the individual, or that it is a by-product of the seasonal sexual condition to which no meaning can be attached. First, there is the relationship with the territory, and this, it seems to me, is a fact of some importance; for if the fighting were merely an exuberant manifestation of sexual emotion, one would expect to find it occurring under all conditions, and not merely under one particular condition in the life of the bird. The hostility is too widespread, however, and too uniform in occurrence for us to suppose that it has no root in the inherited constitution of the bird; and if it served some useful purpose in the past, the instinct might still persist, so long as it were not harmful. Thus the view that the behaviour is vestigial is not perhaps unreasonable. But manifestly it makes no difference whether it be vestigial or a by-product of sexual emotion, 258 whether the battle be fierce or so trivial as to appear to us to be more in the nature of "play," so long as some change in the relative prospects of the opponents is the result.

For us, then, the main consideration lies in the question: Is the behaviour serviceable now in furthering the life of the individual? Whether the evidence which we have examined affords sufficient ground for the belief that the hostility is genuine and has a part to play in the whole scheme of reproduction, each must judge for himself.
259

CHAPTER VII

THE RELATION OF THE TERRITORY TO MIGRATION

Coincident in time with the growth of appropriate conditions in the environment, organic changes take place rendering certain instincts susceptible to stimulation; and the stimulus being applied, the Warbler leaves the country wherein it had passed the winter and finds its way back, with apparently little difficulty, to the district in which it was reared or had previously reared offspring. What is the nature of these changes and of the impulse which is first brought into functional activity; whence comes the stimulus; and what directs the bird on its journey—these are all different aspects of one great problem, the problem of migration. I do not propose to discuss all these various aspects, for indeed I have no suggestions to offer which are in the least likely to be helpful, but I seek rather to ascertain whether the phenomena which we have explored bear any relation to the problem as a whole; whether, that is to say, the competition for territory and all that appertains to it can have 260 supplied the conditions under which, in the process of time, this complex and definite mode of behaviour has evolved.

We are sometimes told that we must seek the origin of migration in the physical changes that have occurred in the ancient history of the earth—in glacial conditions which gradually forced birds to the south, or in the "stability of the water and mobility of the land" which brought about a gradual separation of the feeding area from the breeding area—and which continued for a sufficient length of time to lead to the formation of an instinct, and that the instinct persists because it is serviceable in promoting the welfare of the race. But when we consider the lapse of time, and the changes that must have occurred in the character of the bird population—the appearance of new forms and the disappearance of the old, the ebb and flow of a given species in a given area—and bear in mind that, notwithstanding this, the migratory instinct, if not stronger, is assuredly no less strong, and the volume of migration, if not greater, is assuredly no less; in short, that the whole phenomenon is progressive rather than retrogressive, we shall find the view that the instinct owes its origin to conditions which no longer exist, receives but little encouragement.

I doubt not that, throughout the ages, geological changes have been an important factor in directing or limiting the scope of migration, and moreover are so still; just as 261 climatic changes and the relative abundance or scarcity of enemies have influenced the course of its evolution. These are all contributory factors operating in the external environment. But there are, besides, internal factors which form part of the inherited constitution of the bird, and, being passed on from generation to generation, afford the conditions under which migration is constantly being renewed. It is, I believe, in this field of organic change and relationship that the conditions of origin must be sought.

Just as the moth in passing from the rudimentary to the perfect condition runs through a series of changes, each one of which is marked by a typical behaviour response adjusted to meet some particular circumstance in the external environment, so the annual history of a bird displays an ordered routine, each phase of which can be observed to correspond with one of the successive changes in the environment. In almost every direction, we find that this routine is characterised, in broad outline, by great uniformity; so much so that, providing we know the history of one species, we can forecast with no small degree of certainty the general course of behaviour of other members of the family. But only the *general* course. There is endless variation in just the particular way in which the behaviour is adapted to meet the needs of particular species—the major details may be said to be specific, the minor details varietal.

262 Now it is that part of the behaviour routine which has reference to the relationship between one bird and another upon which, for the time being, I wish to dwell; for the interest that A displays in B is by no means always the same—it changes according to the season, and this change can be observed to be uniform throughout a wide range of species.

In winter, in whatsoever direction we turn, we observe not only that different individuals but that different species also collect together in flocks. And since food at that season is not always easy to obtain, and, moreover, is only to be found in certain situations, which are limited both in number and extent, it would seem that such assemblages are in the main determined by accident. No doubt the abundance or the scarcity of food does determine the movements of birds, and hence to that extent may be held to account for the flocks. But we shall but deceive ourselves if we think that it is the sole or even the principal reason, or that the situation is in no wise affected by internal factors. The behaviour of the individual in relation to the flock bears ample testimony to the presence of a gregarious impulse which derives satisfaction from the fact of close association.

As an illustration, let us take a bird whose movements are easily watched, and in whose hereditary constitution the impulse to which I allude seems to be strongly implanted—the Curlew. When the breeding season is over, Curlew leave the mountain and the moor and 263 return to the coast or tidal estuaries for the remainder of the year. Here, at low water, they find an abundant supply of food—crustaceans amongst the seaweed upon the rocks, and lobworms (*Arenicola piscatorum*) in the mud as the tide advances or recedes. But when the tide is full, they retire to those parts of the shore that remain uncovered—to isolated rocks, or to sand-dunes, or it may even be to pasture-land in the neighbourhood. During this period of repose large numbers of individuals gather together on a comparatively small space of ground. They are not constrained to do so by any shortage of accommodation, nor by any question relative to food, nor, for the matter of that, by any circumstance in the external environment; they are brought together solely, this at least is the impression that one gains, by some inherited impulse working towards that end. And their subsequent course of behaviour tends to confirm that impression. For if we watch the gathering together of the different units of which the flock is composed, and study more particularly the emotional manifestation which accompanies their arrival and departure, we shall find that the coming of a companion arouses some emotion which is expressed by a vocal outburst that sweeps through the flock.

Now each call, and the Curlew has a great variety, is not only peculiar, generally speaking, to certain occasions, but is accompanied by a specific type of behaviour, whence we can infer in broad outline the type of emotion which is aroused. Thus we come to recognise fear, anger, or sexual emotion, by just the particular sound which is emitted. But even if we are going too far in referring particular calls to particular emotions, we can, without a doubt, divide them into two broad categories—those which are pleasurable and those which are the reverse. And we need have no hesitation in placing the particular call to which I allude in the first of these two categories, not only on account of the nature of the sound produced, but because the activities which are aroused are not such as normally accompany irritation. This is well seen if the behaviour of different individuals be closely observed. After resting on one leg for some time, first one and then another is seized with cramp, and running a few yards in an ungainly way, bumps up against its companions as if it had not full control over its movements. Its behaviour produces irritation which is expressed by a vocal outburst, and followed by actions the meaning of which is clear. Moreover, the call is taken up by other individuals and sweeps over part of the flock as does the greeting. But the nature of the cry is entirely different from that which greets the arrival of a companion—humanly speaking it is a passionate and impatient utterance, the height of displeasure. The arrival, then, acts as a stimulus to something in the inherited constitution which is expressed in, and presumably is satisfied by, this vocal outburst; and, since the bird that arrives joins also in the chorus, there is reason to think that the impulse which determines its movements is similar to that which is temporarily aroused in the flock.

Apart, however, from the evidence derived from the affective aspect of the operation of the instinct, the general course of behaviour lends support to the view that the assemblies are determined by internal factors, and are not merely the outcome of circumstances in the external environment. Observe, for example, the manner in which the flock is built up. Single individuals are content to rest alone so long as no assembly is in sight, but they are drawn towards their companions directly the opportunity arises, just as surely as the smaller aggregation is drawn towards the flock; and so, as the flock increases, it gradually absorbs all the lesser flocks and smaller parties, for the greater the flock the greater the attraction seems to be; and different individuals appear to gain some satisfaction from being in close bodily contact with one another.

When the Curlew flies to that part of the mud-flat which is first exposed by the receding tide, and there associates with others, it does not then do so because it has any interest in its fellows, nor because they serve as an attraction, but because it is constrained by hunger—in other words, the association is determined by accident. But when, during periods of repose, it sees a flock, flies to it, and takes up a position in the midst of it, it does so not because suitable accommodation is lacking—not therefore because of external constraint—but because it derives some pleasure from satisfying something in its organic complex. We speak of this behaviour and of the emotion which characterises it as the *gregarious instinct*: by which we mean that the inherited nature of the Curlew, as a tribe, is so constituted that, given the appropriate internal conditions and adequate external stimulation, every individual will respond in a similar manner—that is, the behaviour is primarily determined by racial preparation. This is what we mean by the *gregarious instinct* biologically considered. We may resolve our own experience in relation to the crowd into its simplest constituents, project our own primitive feelings into the Curlew, and say that the bird feels uneasiness in isolation and satisfaction in being one of the flock. But in truth we know nothing, save by analogy, of the correlated psychical state. All the knowledge we possess is derived from a study of the objective aspect of the behaviour, which in simple terms may be expressed thus: the individual is drawn towards its companions; there is a relation between the size of the flock and the strength of the attraction; and all Curlew behave similarly under similar circumstances.

This instinct controls the movements of many birds from early autumn to the commencement of the breeding season. And so powerful is the control that the individual is suppressed and its activities subordinated to the welfare of the community as a whole. Flocks of Waders roam about the tidal estuaries in search of food, and different kinds of Gulls assemble there and preen their feathers or sleep; Warblers alter their mode of life, and in the osier bed, or amongst the elders, seek their food together in peace; Finches, Buntings, Pipits, and Wagtails, though food is everywhere abundant, gather themselves together respectively into bands which, as winter approaches, grow into flocks and even into composite flocks; and as the Warblers leave for the south, so their places are filled by flocks of Thrushes and Finches from the north. In whatever direction we turn, when the days begin to shorten, it is the community, not the individual, that thrusts itself upon our attention; and throughout the winter continues to be the outstanding feature of bird life.

With the approach of the breeding season we witness that remarkable change which I have endeavoured to make clear in the previous chapters—the disintegration of the flock and the reinstatement of the individual. Instead of continuing with the flock, the individual now goes forth to seek the appropriate breeding ground; and having arrived there, is not only content to remain in isolation, but so behaves that isolation is insured. Intolerant of the approach of a stranger, intolerant even of the approach of the very members of the community whose companionship was previously welcomed, it not only fights to maintain the position it has selected, but fights indeed for the possession of ground already occupied, and, until reproduction is completed, asserts its individuality and exercises dominion over its territory. What, then, is the prospective value, biologically considered, of the changing interest that A displays in B, and to what will such changes lead? These are the questions to which we will now direct inquiry.

The annual life-history of a bird is in broad outline conditioned by two powerful and at first sight opposing impulses—the one to live in society, the other to live solitary. But, manifestly, a bird cannot be governed by opposing impulses. It has but one character, within which, according to the season and the circumstances, different impulses predominate. But these impulses, no matter how different they may appear to be, have their respective parts to play in furthering the life of the individual. Hence they cannot oppose, though they may conflict, if the resultant behaviour contributes towards survival.

The majority of birds live to-day in constant danger from predatory species, and that this danger was still greater in bygone ages there can be but little doubt. A curious mode of behaviour of the Curlew, Whimbrel, and Godwit demonstrates this, for it must be the outcome of the necessity for constant watchfulness. Whilst resting with its head turned back and its beak buried in the feathers of the mantle, the bird constantly moves the axis of its body, so that an observer, if placed in a direct line 269 behind it, sees at one moment the right eye and at another the left. No movement of the feet or of the legs is perceptible, and the shifting of the body continues whether the eyes are open or closed. This body movement enables the bird to survey a much larger area of ground than it would otherwise be capable of doing, and thus adds to its security. As far as my experience goes, the movement is less evident amongst the members of a flock than when an individual is resting alone, or even with a few companions, which may be due to the fact that since some members are always awake and watchful, a bird of prey would have more difficulty in approaching a flock unawares than it would have in approaching a single individual. With the greatest ease a Sparrow-Hawk can pick up a Thrush as it feeds on the meadow by itself, but if it attempts to seize one of a flock, the chances are that its approach is signalled and that its prey escapes. And not only do the different members give warning one to another of the approach of danger, but they also combine to harass or even to drive away an enemy. So that there can be no doubt that the gregarious instinct is serviceable in promoting the welfare of the race, and has, as its end, the preservation of the individual in order that it may take its share at the appropriate time in procreating its kind.

In winter, then, the individual loses its individuality and is subordinated to the welfare of the community, whilst in spring it regains 270 its individuality, and all its inherited instincts which then come into operation lead to its isolation from the flock. The impulse to seek isolation is dependent upon internal organic conditions which are peculiar to a certain season; whereas the gregarious impulse depends upon internal organic conditions which inhere at all times, though its functioning is inhibited by the functioning of the former impulse. The evidence which leads to this conclusion is to be found in the fact that a male often deserts its territory temporarily and joins the flock, where it remains at peace with its companions—an aspect of behaviour which we have discussed on various occasions. The former impulse becomes dominant in the spring owing to its innately superior strength; the latter becomes dominant in the autumn because the organic condition which determines the functioning of the former then subsides. The impulse to seek the appropriate breeding ground and to dwell there would seem to be the strongest of all the impulses save one—the sexual. When, however, I speak of the sexual, I refer to the actual discharge of the sexual function, which is the consummation of the whole process. But the territory and all that appertains to it is part of that process—the search for the breeding ground, the dwelling there, and the intolerance of intrusion are but different stages, each one of which must have an impulse peculiar to it; and since the completion of the sexual act can only be 271 successfully accomplished providing that success is attained at every stage, the probability is that, of the impulses concerned, one is neither more powerful nor less powerful than another.

So that we have two impulses operating at different seasons and guiding the behaviour into widely divergent channels. But though the proximate end to which the behaviour is directed is apparently different, there are not two biological ends in view, but one—the attainment of reproduction; and the changes that we witness are not contrary but complementary, and their prospective value lies in the circumstance that they contribute towards the preservation of the race.

If, then, every male is driven by inherited impulse to seek the appropriate breeding ground each recurring season; if, having arrived there, it is driven to seek a position of its own; if, in order to secure isolation it is obliged to attack other males or to ward off the attacks of intruders; if, in short, success can only be attained providing that the inherited nature is so adjusted that the bird can accomplish all that is here demanded—what will be the general result? That the individual will rear its offspring in safety and that they will inherit the peculiarities of their parents, enabling them, in their turn, to procreate their kind; all this will certainly follow. We are not concerned, however, at the moment, with the direct effect upon the individual, but with the consequences that will accrue to the species as a whole.

272 Now certain facts are presented to observation which enable us not only to understand the nature of the change that is wrought in the history of the species, but to foreshadow, with no small degree of certainty, the extent of that change. I suppose that it has come within the experience of most of us to observe, at one time or another, the ebb and flow of a given species in a given district. Some favourite haunt is deserted for a year, or for a term of years, and is then revisited; or, if it is always occupied, the number of inhabitants fluctuates—plenty of pairs in this season, only a few in that. Many intricate relationships, both external and internal, contribute towards this state of affairs.

Fluctuation in a downward direction, or temporary extinction, is brought about by changes in the physical world, by changes in the available supply of food, by the increase of enemies, or by adverse climatic conditions; whilst fluctuation in an upward direction, though due indirectly to a combination of circumstances in the external world favourable to the survival of large numbers of individuals, is directly determined by the impulse to seek isolation. As individuals of different species establish themselves, and form kingdoms and lesser kingdoms, we can watch the gradual quickening into life of moorland and forest and we can observe the manner in which it all comes to pass. Males that for weeks or months have lived in society, drifting from locality to locality according to the abundance of food or its 273 scarcity, now set forth alone and settle first here and then there in search of isolation. Lapwings settle in the water meadows, and, finding themselves forestalled, pass on in search of other ground; Blackbirds arrive in a coppice or in a hedgerow and, meeting with opposition, disappear; and the Curlew, wandering with no fixed abode but apparently with a fixity of purpose, searches out the moorland where it can find the particular environmental conditions to which its inherited nature will respond. In fact, wherever we choose to look, we can observe in a general way the gradual appropriation of breeding ground; and if we fix our attention upon particular males, we can watch the method by which success or failure is achieved.

On more than one occasion I have watched the efforts of Reed-Buntings to appropriate territories in a marsh that was already inhabited. Sometimes their efforts met with success, at other times with failure. In the former case, the males, whose ground was intruded upon, were severally forced to yield part of their holding and were thus left in possession of a smaller area. The success of the intruder seemed to depend upon persistent determination, rather than upon superior skill in battle. Recently I had an opportunity of observing the intrusion of a male Willow-Warbler upon ground already occupied. By persistent effort it succeeded in appropriating one half of the territory of its rival. The intruder occupied some trees on the 274 outskirts of the territory it was invading, and used them as a base from which it made repeated efforts to enter the ground of its rival. These efforts were time after time frustrated. No sooner did it leave its base than it was seen and intercepted, or else attacked; and no matter from which direction it attempted to effect an entrance, its efforts, for a time, were all to no purpose. The fighting was of a determined character, and after each attack the owner of the territory showed signs of great excitement, and, sitting upright upon a branch, spread and waved its wings, which is the specific emotional manifestation during the period of sexual activity. Eventually the intruding male succeeded by persistent effort in appropriating part of the occupied ground.

Thus we can actually witness the efforts of the individual to isolate itself from members of its own kind, and can observe the immediate consequences that follow from success or from failure. And from these consequences we can infer that, within a certain range but in accordance with the relative abundance of the species that dwell in it, every corner of the available breeding ground will be explored and every situation that evokes the appropriate response will be occupied. Moreover, since the annual dispersion is not merely a repetition in this season of that which occurred in a previous one, a progressive increase in the area occupied will follow. Yet, if the majority of species desert their breeding ground so soon as reproduction is 275 ended, how can this be? An answer to the question will be found in the fact that a bird has an innate capacity to return to the neighbourhood of its birthplace, or to the place wherein it had previously reared offspring—which means that the results of prior process persist as the basis and starting-point of subsequent process.

Bearing then in mind that the seeming peace in bird life around us in the spring is but the expression of transitory adjustments in the distribution of individuals and of species; bearing in mind how widespread is the search for isolation each recurring season, how frequently the search leads to competition and competition to failure, and how failure implies a renewal of the search; bearing in mind that situations, which appear to be eminently suitable for breeding purposes, are passed by year after year and remain unoccupied, just because, for reasons which have yet to be ascertained, the environment fails to supply some condition which is essential if the inherited nature of the bird is to respond—can there be any doubt that the general result of the functioning of the disposition will be expansion; or, since no limit is placed upon it from within but only from without—that is, by unfavourable circumstances in the external world, that the expansion will not merely be in one direction but in every direction?

If now, when reproduction is ended, all the impulses relating to it die away, and the 276 gregarious instinct again predominates, what are the consequences to which this change will lead? Just as the consequences which flow from the functioning of the former impulse are accessible to observation, so likewise can we observe the change that is wrought by the latter impulse. The process is a gradual one. Less and less attention is paid by the individual to intruders, more and more is it disposed to pass beyond its accustomed limits. Little by little, accompanied by its young or without them, as the case may be, the bird deserts its territory and wanders out into the wilderness. Here it associates with others, and finds in them a new interest and, I doubt not, a new enjoyment. All this we can observe as it takes place. But just as there is an innate capacity to seek, in the spring, the place where the pleasures of breeding had formerly been enjoyed, so we are bound to infer the existence in the adult of an innate capacity to revisit the former area of association; and this capacity will strengthen and confirm the gregarious instinct and set the direction of the general course of movement.

We have seen, then, that the interest displayed by one bird in another changes with the seasons; we have seen that it is so modified as to be in useful relation to different environmental circumstances; as far as possible we have traced out the consequences, and have reached the conclusion that the change of behaviour must, on the one hand, lead to expansion, and on the other, to contraction; 277 and we have seen that this conclusion is in accord with the facts of observation—that is the general result of our inquiry into the functioning of the two powerful impulses, the impulse associated with the disposition to secure a territory and the gregarious impulse.

The phenomenon of migration embraces a number of separate problems, each one of which presents features of great interest and of still greater difficulty. On some of these problems I do not intend to touch; I seek only to ascertain whether the impulses that are concerned in the securing of a territory, and in the search for society, bear any relation to the problem as a whole. I hold that the origin of migration is not to be found merely in conditions peculiar to a remote past, but that the conditions inhere in the organic complex of the bird, and are thus handed down from generation to generation. Starting with this assumption I examined the behaviour which normally accompanies the seasonal life-history of the individual, and found, in that behaviour, manifestations of cyclical change leading to definite biological consequences. I now propose to inquire whether those consequences are such as might, in the course of time, give rise to the seasonal change of abode.

We are apt to think of migration in terms of the Warbler that enlivens our hedgerows in the spring after travelling hundreds of miles from the south, or of the Redwing that comes from 278 the far north and seeks its food during the winter on the meadows, or perhaps of the American Golden Plover that each year covers a vast expanse of ocean in its journey from its breeding ground. The length of the distance strikes the imagination and constrains us to focus attention upon the extremes.

But migration is of much wider significance than is here represented. I sit beside the River Severn in April and watch Swallows, Tree-Pipits, and Yellow Wagtails passing in twos and threes, in small parties, or it may be in small flocks; and I observe that while some establish themselves in the neighbourhood, others pass on. Or I watch Herring-Gulls returning to the breeding station at Bolt Head, an endless stream of individuals coming from the east as far as eye can reach; following them for some miles inland I see them still, first as specks upon the horizon, then passing beside me as they beat their way slowly against the strong south-westerly winds, and finally disappearing from view in the direction of the cliffs. Or again, I watch Buntings and Finches deserting the flock and seeking stations in the marsh, or amongst the furze-bushes on the common, or in the spinneys. In each case the proximate end of the behaviour is alike—wherein then lies the difference? Only in the distance which separates the territory from the area in which the birds formerly associated. And intermediate between the extremes, I doubt not, if we had a sufficient body of observations, that we should 279 find numerous gradations, the lesser merging step by step into the greater. Is the Swallow a migrant and the Herring-Gull not; is the Tree-Pipit a migrant and the Bunting not; must a bird cross many miles of sea or of land before it can be considered a migrant; is the length of the distance traversed a criterion of migration? Surely not. The distance traversed is merely a collateral consequence of the process as a whole.

The annual life-history of a bird presents, as we have seen, two distinct phases—the one in which the individual dominates the situation, the other in which it is subordinated to the welfare of the community. Let us take these two phases separately and endeavour to see how they may have influenced the seasonal movements; and first let us take the more important of the two, namely that one which is directly concerned in the continuance of the race.

In this phase we must consider the three factors to which allusion has already been made:—(1) the internal impulse, (2) the innate ability to return to the former breeding ground, (3) the conditions in the external environment. These three work in close relation and, as I shall endeavour to show, lead to important results.

(1) If there were nothing in the inherited nature beyond an impulse to seek the breeding ground, if, that is to say, when the appropriate locality were reached, the bird took no further interest in the developing situation, the attainment of reproduction would become largely a 280 matter of chance. A male in a congested district, having no incentive to seek fresh ground, would remain inactive until a female happened to cross its path and stimulate its sexual impulse, when its activity would take another form. Hence some districts would be over-populated, whilst others would remain unexplored. But the system of reproduction does not consist merely of a search for the breeding ground, and of the discharge of the sexual function; it is a much more complex business, yet withal more complete. Nothing is left to chance; the end is attained step by step; and each successive stage marks the appearance of some specific factor which contributes towards the success of the whole. We start with the appropriate organic condition under which, when adequate stimulation is provided, the disposition to secure a territory comes into functional activity. Within the field of this disposition we can distinguish certain specific impulses. In sequential order we have the impulse to seek the breeding ground; the appropriate situation which gives rise to an impulse to dwell in it; and the act of establishment which supplies the condition under which the impulse to drive away intruders is rendered susceptible to stimulation. Grouping these impulses, for the convenience of treatment, under one general heading, I speak of an impulse to seek isolation. It implies some kind of action

with some kind of change as its correlated effect; and from it there flows a ceaseless energy directed towards a definite end which for us, who can perceive its prospective value, is isolation in an appropriate environment. The emphasis here is on "isolation," for it involves competition, and there cannot be competition without some change in the relative positions occupied by different individuals; so that in each recurring season there will be not only a re-arrangement of ground formerly occupied but an arrangement of ground formerly deserted.

(2) That the older birds return to the locality wherein they had formerly reared offspring, and the younger to the neighbourhood of their birthplace, was always deemed probable. But in recent years evidence which cannot be rebutted has been supplied by the marking of birds. This evidence, details of which can be found in the summary of results published annually by Mr. Witherby in *British Birds*, demonstrates that the adult frequently returns not only to the same locality in which it formerly bred, but even to the same station; that it does so year after year; that this mode of behaviour is not peculiar to one sex; and that many of the young breed in the locality in which they were reared. Such being well-established facts, we can infer the existence of an innate ability to revisit the place wherein the enjoyment of breeding, or of birth, had formerly been experienced. Of its nature we know little or nothing. It would almost seem as if there must be some recollection of past enjoyment, but all that can be definitely asserted is—that past experience somehow becomes ingrained in the life of the individual and determines present behaviour. What, however, is of importance to us at the moment is not the *ad hoc* nature of the bird, but the biological consequences to which the behaviour leads. For if, on the average, individuals return to their former haunts, it follows that the annual dispersion will not be merely a repetition in this season of that which had occurred in a previous one, but that the little added this year will become the basis for further additions in the next. The innate ability is handed down from generation to generation, and, in so far as it contributes to success, is fostered and developed by selection; and the modifications of behaviour to which it leads, since the results of prior process in the parent persist as the basis and starting-point of subsequent process in the offspring may in a sense also be said to be handed down.

(3) The conditions in the external world may be organic or inorganic. By organic I mean the conditions which depend upon the number of competitors or enemies by which a bird is surrounded. The competitors may include other species which require a similar environment; and the enemies, species which prey upon it, or animals which take its young or its eggs. They vary in different seasons, in different districts, and in nature and extent—the success of one species leads to the failure of another, and the multiplication of the Jay or of the Magpie robs us of many a songster.

By inorganic I refer to the changes in the climate and in the surface of the earth. The nourishment of the young depends upon a regular supply of food, and the supply of food depends upon the climate which alters in different periods; in one decade the temperature falls below, whilst in another it rises above, the normal, and, as the insect life fluctuates, so there is fluctuation in the bird population. The changes in the surface of the earth are manifold. Little by little the alder (*Alnus glutinosa*) overspreads the marsh. Young shoots spring up here and there, in a few years grow into bushes, and in a few more years are trees; and the dense masses of rush which seemed to choke their growth, yielding their position of importance, slowly disappear. And where formerly the *Orchis latifolia*, *Orchis mascula*, and *Juncus communis* grew in mingled confusion, nothing but water, moss, and the spreading roots of alder cover the ground. As the rush disappears, many birds that for generations have inhabited that marsh must seek accommodation elsewhere. Ancient breeding haunts thus disappear, new ones come into being, and even those which appear to be permanent are almost imperceptibly changing.

Now the bird inherits a nervous system, which works under internal excitation and external stimulation. Given the appropriate organic condition and adequate stimulation, and the impulse to seek isolation comes into functional activity. What the organic condition is and how it arises we do not exactly know; all we know is that organic changes do take place in the breeding season, that these changes profoundly modify character, and that they correspond with the seasonal growth of the sexual organs. And with regard to the question of stimulation, we have again to confess to much ignorance, although certain facts are presented to observation which seem to indicate the direction in which the stimulus lies. For example, it is well known that abnormal climatic conditions influence behaviour; we see migrants retracing their flight along the very course they travelled a short time previously—driven headlong by the blizzard, that at least is what we say. But if the wind, instead of being cold and from the north, is warm and from the west, do they retrace their flight? I have not found it so. And if there be no wind and the temperature is low, are they still affected? Again, I have not found it so. When, as we commonly say, they fly before the storm, some change takes place in their organic complex, some new impulse receives stimulation or the former one lacks it. If, after Lapwings have established themselves in their territories, the weather becomes exceptionally severe, the birds collect together again in flocks and revert to their winter routine; and under similar circumstances, Buntings fail to sing and temporarily desert their territories. In such cases it is clear that the impulse to seek isolation ceases for a time to dominate the situation. The inference, therefore, is that atmospheric changes bear some relation to the functioning of the instinct; but whether it be temperature, or humidity, or the direction and velocity of the wind, or a combination of two or more of these factors that supplies the stimulus, we cannot tell.

The appropriate organic condition and the stimulus have then still to be determined, and we must pursue our inquiry from the point at which the impulse comes into functional activity. We will take a simple case, and one free from complication.

Let us suppose that there is an area bereft of bird life, if it can be so imagined, but in proximity to other inhabited areas. Into this area, whilst in search of isolation, let us imagine that a Yellow Bunting finds its way. After the manner of its race it establishes a territory and occupies, let us say at a low computation, half an acre of ground. It then obtains a mate, breeds, and rears offspring, two of which we will assume are males. Reproduction ended, the birds desert the area, and in the following spring, when the impulse again asserts itself, parents and offspring seek again their former haunts. We now have three males, each of which occupies half an acre, and each of which rears two offspring—that is the position at the close of the second year. In the third year the number will have increased to nine and the area occupied to 4½ acres; and so on in succeeding years, until by the beginning of the eleventh year, we have 59,048 Yellow Buntings occupying 29,524½ acres or 46 square miles. This, then, will be the result of the operation of the impulse, providing that all the individuals survive and that no complications supervene.

But of course complications are numerous, some of which retard while others accelerate the rate of expansion. These complications arise from various sources—in the first place from natural enemies which prey upon the birds or upon their eggs; in the next place from climate which, if it happens to be unfavourable, may mean that food is scarce and that only a small percentage of the young survive; and lastly from rivals—and by rivals I mean closely related forms that require a similar station and similar food—which, by occupying available ground, may check expansion, or, by forcing a continuation of the search, may widen it.

Now when individuals fail as many do fail in their initial attempt to secure territory, the activity of the impulse still persists, and there is no control over the direction in which the bird continues to wander whilst in search of its end. Some therefore seek in this direction, others in that; some wander inwards into inhabited areas and fail to find accommodation, or, according to the relative strength of their impulse, perhaps succeed and so set free a new competitor, others wander outwards into country uninhabited by the species. These latter we will call "pioneers." They may find accommodation within a comparatively short distance of their base, or they may come into competition with rivals and fail, not necessarily on account of any congenital weakness of ability, but because being warned by an alien song, they may be precluded from coming into contact with just the environing conditions which can supply the stimulus and allow behaviour to run its further course—and so be obliged to extend their search into remoter districts. But it must not be overlooked that they will be placed in a most advantageous position so far as the attainment of reproduction is concerned. In their search for territory they will meet with little opposition and will be free to select whatsoever ground they will; and be free also from intrusion by neighbouring males, which is so frequent in occurrence and continues for so long in congested areas. Moreover, in thinly populated districts, the pressure upon the available means of support will not be so great, neither will natural enemies be so plentiful; and since the offspring, guided by prior experience, return to the neighbourhood of their birthplace, the advantages thus gained will be shared by the succeeding generation. It follows, then, that the range of a species will not always be continuous, will not, that is to say, proceed by a series of successive steps, but that sometimes in this direction and at other times in that, the chain of territories will be interrupted and different individuals separated by distances of greater or lesser extent. New colonies will thus come into being; and as the unlimited increase of the population over limited areas gradually reintroduces into them the struggle for territory, new centres of distribution, where the process will repeat itself and from which expansion will proceed afresh, will be formed. Hence, though it is clearly impossible for the progeny of one pair of Yellow Buntings to overspread the whole of the 46 square miles, it is by no means impossible for the limits of their range to exceed even those limits within the eleven years.

To sum up our knowledge regarding this phase. Of the organic condition which renders the impulse responsive to stimulation we know very little; and though certain facts of observation seem to indicate the direction in which the stimulus is to be found, we must here again confess to much ignorance. So far as can be seen, however, the impulse to seek isolation with its correlative territory, leads to constant modification in the breeding range of most species. The occupation of the small space of ground which each individual requires, the extent of which has been gradually adjusted to suit the needs of different species, results in expansion not only in one direction but in every direction, and not only in one season but in every season. And if there were no complications in the external world this expansion would proceed, as we have seen, with astonishing rapidity. But complications, some of which are favourable and others unfavourable, are numerous, and it is difficult to estimate their importance or to indicate their precise effect; the former, however, accelerate the rate of expansion, whilst the latter retard it. Those individuals that wander outwards and seek territory on the outskirts of the range we have called "pioneers." They will have advantages over others that, wandering inwards, seek isolation in congested districts, and will succeed where the latter fail; and since there is in the young an innate ability to return to the district wherein they were reared, the advantages so gained may be said to be handed on from generation to generation.

Let us now turn to the contra-phase, and endeavour to ascertain whether the gregarious instinct bears any relation to the seasonal desertion of the breeding ground. The conclusion at which we have already arrived regarding this instinct is that it forms part of the inherited nature of most species; that its functioning is suppressed when a bird is actually in occupation of a territory; and that it is serviceable in promoting the welfare of the individual. We cannot of course observe the instinct. What we observe, when reproduction is ended, is a change in the relations of different individuals; instead of arousing mutual hostility, they attract one another, from which we infer the existence of something which determines their conduct, and this "something" we speak of as an instinct.

To what does this change lead? Let us suppose that there is an area inhabited by one 290 species; that the number of inhabitants has reached the maximum that the means of sustenance will allow; and that the season of reproduction is drawing to a close. The position will then be as follows. All the available breeding ground is divided into territories; each territory is occupied by one unit, the family, and each individual is able to fend for itself; changes both internal and external begin to take place, the gregarious instinct comes into functional operation, and the supply of food diminishes—that roughly is the position. The internal factor operates so that the sight of this individual or the call of that, instead of evoking hostility as heretofore and keeping different units apart, proves now an irresistible attraction; so that in place of a number of individuals evenly dispersed over the whole of this area, a small number of flocks of various dimensions are stationed at certain points, which points are determined partly by experience, partly by the supply of food, and partly by accident. This implies for each individual some movement in some direction. But since the population of this imaginary area has reached the maximum, and the supply of food, though limited in distribution, is nevertheless plentiful, such movements will be irregular and will proceed in no definite direction.

Now let us suppose that the breeding range extends and that fresh ground is occupied by pioneers. When reproduction and the rearing of broods are ended and the gregarious instinct 291 becomes dominant, these pioneers, or at least some of them, will revisit the area wherein formerly they associated with companions. Their offspring, however, though they will have the inherited impulse and the innate tendency, will not have the experience; how then will they behave? There can be no doubt that some will accompany the older birds, and, being led by them, will share the experience of a former generation; nor any question that others will collect together in the neighbourhood of their birthplace and, if their impulse is satisfied, will remain there so long as food is to be found. Thus the gregarious instinct, working in close relation with acquired experience, will on the one hand lead to the formation of organised movements in certain directions, whilst on the other it will lead to the formation of new areas of association which will follow in the wake of the expansion.

We have assumed, in the imaginary case which we have just taken, that the conditions in the external world are such as enable the birds to endure throughout the year—in short, that there are no complications regarding the supply of food. But we must bear in mind that so long as conditions are favourable during the period of reproduction, which is of short duration, the breeding range can continue to expand, and that therefore, in the course of centuries, regions will come to be occupied wherein, owing to alternations of climate or physical changes in the surface of the earth, 292 food will be impossible, or at any rate difficult to obtain at certain seasons. Hence there will come a time when the area of association ceases to follow in the wake of the expansion, and the breeding area begins to diverge from the subsistence area.

How, then, is the gulf between these two areas to be bridged? We can of course say that those individuals which, in virtue of some slight variation of hereditary tendency, return to regions where food is plentiful will survive; whilst others, less well endowed, will perish. We can state the position in some such general terms, and doubtless there would be truth in the statement, but it does not carry us far; we wish to know more of the nature of the tendency, and of the manner in which it has evolved. Well now, in this new situation which arises, two things are apparent—that the struggle for existence becomes a struggle for the means of subsistence, and that anything in the inherited constitution of the bird which can be organised to subserve the biological end in view becomes of selection value. So long as food can always be procured in the new areas of association, the individuals that behave in accordance with ancestral routine gain thereby no particular advantage; but directly the breeding range extends into regions where the supply fluctuates, traditional experience becomes a factor in survival, and those individuals that come under its influence will, on the average, be more likely to endure and so 293 to procreate their kind and maintain the tradition. Let it once be granted that there is an innate capacity to retain in later phases of routine the experience gained in earlier phases, and it is difficult to see how traditional guidance can be refused recognition as a factor in the developing situation. But only *a* factor, and by no means the most important one; for observation has shown that the young are capable of performing the return journey without guidance. Something therefore *is* inherited, some impulse which comes into functional activity at a specified time, and leads the bird to set forth in a given direction.

There are no grounds for supposing that the experience of one generation forms any part of the hereditary equipment of subsequent generations. In what direction then are we to look for the congenital factor? What is given is an inherited tendency to co-operation and mutual help, and an innate capacity to make use of the results of experience. The inherited tendency, as we have seen, leads on the one hand to the formation of new areas of association, whilst on the other, since it is the means of bringing isolated individuals into contact, it leads to experience being handed on from generation to generation, which, in its turn, results in a certain amount of backward movement along the line of expansion. It forms part of the hereditary equipment of many species, and is serviceable in promoting the welfare of the individual. Moreover, there is 294 reason to believe that its origin dates back to an early period in the evolution of the higher forms of life; and if in the subsequent course of evolution it could have been so organised as to serve a double purpose, so much the more reason would there have been for its survival. In what does the instinct consist? Is it merely that the sight of this individual or the call of that proves at some particular moment an irresistible attraction, or does the appropriate organic condition give rise, as is generally supposed, to some preceding state of uneasiness? In the former case, the temporarily isolated individual or colony would have but little chance of sharing in the benefits which mutual association confers upon the associates; in the latter, the feeling of discomfort would lead to restlessness, and would thus bring the bird into touch with the environing circumstances under which instinctive behaviour could run its further course. So that it is probable that the movements of each individual, prior to its becoming a unit in the flock, are not accidental but are determined in some measure by racial preparation.

Now if the fundamental assumption of the doctrine of the struggle for existence be true, the gregarious instinct will not be quite alike in all the members of different broods, nor even in each member of the same brood; that is, variation will occur in all possible directions. And we shall not, I think, exceed the limits of probability if we assume that different individuals 295 vary in the persistency with which they strive to attain their unknown end, and in the direction in which they travel in pursuit of it. So that in each generation they will fall into three classes: (1) those which are inert, (2) those which wander along the line of expansion, (3) those which wander in other directions. If then the struggle for life at this particular juncture in the evolution of the breeding range is a struggle for the means of subsistence, the members of these three classes will not be in a like satisfactory position so far as the competition for food is concerned. Those in the first class—*i.e.*, those in which the activity feelings are weak—will neither gain the benefits which arise from mutual help, nor will they have much prospect of enduring through the season of scarcity. Those in the third class will, it is true, derive some assistance one from another, and so be in a better position to discover what food may be available; but inasmuch as they will remain in regions where the climate alternates and the supply of food is liable to fall below the minimum required, the chances are that a high percentage will fail in the struggle for existence. We come now to those in the second class, and it is upon them that I wish more particularly to focus attention. The initial movement in their case will be in the direction from which outward expansion has all along taken place. Within a comparatively short distance they will reach districts where the species is plentiful, and here, associating with others that have some traditional 296 experience, they will be guided by them and will find themselves in regions where food is plentiful. Hence in each generation those will survive that, owing to some congenital variation of their instinct, seek satisfaction for their impulse in a direction which brings them under the influence of tradition. And though at first but slight and not in themselves of survival value, such variations, since they coincide with modifications of behaviour due to acquired experience, will be preserved and in the process of time so accumulated as to be capable of determining the direction and extent of the movement.

But the young Cuckoo deserts this country many weeks after its parents, and there is no reason to suppose that it lives in society when eventually its destination is reached; and the young Falcon passes to the south, and is certainly not gregarious—how then can we explain their behaviour in terms of something which they show no signs of possessing? I do not wish to make light of a difficulty which admittedly, at first sight, is a grave objection to the view that the gregarious instinct has been operative in the manner here claimed for it. It must, however, be borne in mind that this instinct, though originally developed to serve the purpose of mutual protection, supplies the material upon which evolution works when the extension of the breeding range creates a situation requiring readjustment on the part of the organism to new conditions of life; and that 297 those variations which can be so modified as to be in useful relation to the new environmental circumstances are seized upon by natural selection and, being transmitted, form the foundation of a specific inherited response, no longer dependent upon, though operating in close relation with the primitive response whence originally it sprang. Thus the primordial instinct becomes so organised as to serve a secondary purpose, that of rendering secure a means of access to a certain food supply. In the course of evolution species were bound to arise which, owing to some peculiar conditions, derived greater advantage from living solitary than from living in society. Does it then follow, because such species manifest no inclination to live in society, that the instinct never has played any part in their lives? Or because the primary purpose has lapsed, does it follow that the secondary no longer exists?

Let me recapitulate the principal considerations which I have discussed in this chapter.

Though I have been advancing a theory, and though I have taken much for granted, yet it will, I think, be admitted that both the theory and what has been taken for granted rest on observational grounds. As our starting-point we have a bird whose inherited nature alternates according to the season, and in whose nature we can distinguish two contra-phases—the one to live in society, the other to live solitary. While both have their part to play in furthering the life of the individual, for biological interpretation there is only one end, the prospective value of which is the continuance of the race. We may say that the latter phase is the more important of the two because it is directly concerned with reproduction. But we shall make a great mistake if we attach peculiar importance to one phase, or to one mode of behaviour within that phase, or to one action within that mode of behaviour; for if there is one thing certain it is that the whole is an inter-related whole in which each part depends for its success upon that which precedes it.

In that phase in which the territory is the central feature of the situation, the struggle for existence is in operation in its acutest form; all the congenital and acquired capacities of the bird—pugnacity, song, capacity to utilise in later phases the experience gained in prior phases, all these are organised to subserve an end—a proximate end—which in its simplest terms may be described as "isolation." Isolation is then the first step in the process of reproduction, and any individual that fails to make it good, fails to procreate its kind. But isolation implies separation, and the degree of separation varies in different species, from the few square feet of cliff required by the Guillemot to the few square miles of barren moor over which the Peregrine exercises dominion. One species must occupy sufficient ground to enable it to secure food for its young; another requires sufficient, but no more, upon which to deposit its egg; and a third must secure a position for its nest within the community. Hence it follows that the degree of separation varies with the conditions of existence. Since, however, the conditions in the external world are constantly changing according to the relative abundance or scarcity of enemies, the rise or fall of rivals, the physical changes in the earth's surface, and the alterations of climate, it is clear that isolation can only be obtained with difficulty, and that the competition for it must be severe. Some individuals therefore fail to breed, whilst others, perhaps because their impulse is stronger, persevere and seek stations elsewhere. What are their prospects of finding them? By extending the field of their activities, they will wander into districts remote from the scene of competition, districts where not only food is plentiful but where enemies and rivals are scarce; and to these pioneers, if to any, success in reproduction will most certainly be assured. But not only is it they who will benefit; their offspring also, when the time comes for them to take their part in the maintenance of the race, will share in the success of their parents, for even though they may not escape competition from individuals of closely related forms, they will meet with but little from those of their own kind. Now species which live throughout the year in the vicinity of their territory are comparatively few, the majority are obliged to wander in search of food so soon as reproduction is ended, and their behaviour is determined not only by its abundance or scarcity, but also by the powerful gregarious impulse which waxes in proportion as the instincts connected with reproduction wane. If, then, when the sexual instinct again becomes predominant, the experience of the former season nowise affects their movements, little or no progress will be made in the expansion of the range. But just as a certain entrance into the bush and pathway through it, when once made use of in the process of building, becomes so firmly established as to form the sole highway to and from the nest, so likewise, when the impulse to seek isolation repeats itself, the bird is constrained to seek the neighbourhood wherein it had experienced the enjoyment of breeding or of birth. Thus the little that is added one year becomes the basis for further additions in the next, and new centres of distribution are continually being formed from which expansion proceeds anew.

Now as the range gradually extends into regions where the climate alternates and food at certain seasons is consequently scarce, the distance between the customary area of association and that of reproduction must perforce widen. The question then arises: How will the young that have no experience find their way to regions wherein they can endure? The forces which may have been organised to subserve the end in view are three: (1) Acquired experience, (2) tradition, (3) the gregarious instinct. The pioneer that carries the range a little further forward starts from a base where it has associated with companions and found food plentiful; and when the impulse to live in society again asserts itself, it not only repeats its former experience but hands on the habit thus acquired to those of the next generation that happen to accompany it. Granting, however, that by successive increments in the distance traversed, traditional guidance may in time accomplish much, it cannot account for all the known facts, it cannot at any rate explain the fact that in some cases the inexperienced offspring finds its way to the food area without guidance. Something, therefore, *is* inherited. And my suggestion is this: That the gregarious instinct, the ancient origin of which we can infer from its manifestation in so many and diverse forms of life, supplies the material upon which evolution works; that variations of the initial impulse, at first slight and not in themselves of selection value, in so far as they coincide in direction with modifications of procedure due to experience or tradition, are preserved; and that, in the process of time, they are so accumulated as to form a specific congenital endowment determining a definite mode of behaviour.

FOOTNOTES:

1 June 1915, R. M. Barrington.
2 *Dictionary of Birds*, p. 556.
3 *Social Psychology*.
4 *Manual of Psychology*.
5 *Ibis*, April 1918.
6 *Zoologist*, 1912, p. 327.

INDEX

Acquired experience, 300
Adjustments, transitory, of distribution, 275
Alarm notes, 119
Arrival, advantages and disadvantages of late, 33-44
Assemblies in winter, 262, 263
Assembly grounds, 173
Attainment of reproduction, 171

Barrington, R. M., on the sex of migrants, 25
Battle between two male Cuckoos, 82
—— between two Moor-Hens, 86, 92, 93, 94
—— —— Pied Wagtails, 86
—— —— Raven and Buzzard, 217
—— —— Raven and Peregrine, 216
law of, 13, 19
Behaviour routine, 262
—— sexual, 3
Bickerings, 96
Birthplace, return to, 43, 50
Blackbird, 87, 182, 222, 244
Blackcap, 81, 156, 224, 230
Black Grouse, 63
Black-tailed Godwit, 53
Boundaries, 1, 5
—— conflicts for retention of, 7, 62
—— disputes as to, 1
Brambling, 124
Breeding ground, search for appropriate, 270, 271
—— range, extension of, 291-92
—— site, acquirement of, 3
—— stations, evolution of, 15-19
—— —— repeatedly visited long before nesting-time, 64
—— territory, 2, 3, 7
—— —— evolution of, 18
—— —— foundation of, 7
—— —— innate capacity to return to former, 279-81
Bridled Guillemot, 64
Brooding, 180
—— impulse, 191
Bunting, Cirl, 28, 140
—— Corn, 28
—— Reed, 28, 68, 69, 85, 104, 132, 158, 160, 244
—— Yellow, 28, 30, 47, 64, 140, 159, 162, 183, 187, 188, 189, 235, 236, 286
Buzzard, 217

Capacity, innate, to return to former breeding territory, 279-81
Carrion Crow, 226
Chaffinch, 28, 31, 32, 33, 45, 87, 103, 156, 159, 235, 236, 244
—— Donegal, 160 303 Change of breeding quarters owing to unsuitableness, 50
Chiffchaff, 49, 51, 80, 139, 140, 221, 224, 244
Cirl Bunting, 28, 140
Clarke, W. Eagle, *Studies in Bird Migration*, 24
Cleanliness of nest, 180
Cliff-breeding species, 63
Climatic changes, alteration of routine due to, 284
—— changes, food dependent on, 283
—— conditions, influence of, 20
Communities, 202
—— birds after breeding-season remain in, 265-67
Competition, female, for males, 13
Complexity of strife, 84-85
Conflicts between males during the mating period, 74, 86
—— between males during the nesting period, 87
—— for areas, 10, 11, 13, 62
—— of Ruff, 54
—— sexual, 10
Congenital disposition, 135
Contests between males for possession of females, 80
Coot, 61
Corn-Bunting, 28
Corncrake, 39
Crow, Carrion, 226, 227
Crow, Hooded, 202
Cuckoo, 52, 82, 144, 296
—— restricted breeding area, 52
Curlew, 119, 138, 140, 250, 262, 263, 265, 273

Danger warnings, 269
Darwin, C., *Descent of Man*, 35
—— on the arrival of males before females, 35
Defence of territory, 6
Development, sexual, 6
Disposition, congenital, 135
—— functioning of, 74
—— inherited, 5
—— to defend the territory, 73-118
—— to mate, 27

—— to remain in a particular place in a particular environment, 6
—— to secure a territory, 6, 20-72
Distribution, adjustment of, 275
Dove, Turtle, 126, 232
Dunlin, 250

Emotional behaviour, 53, 82, 114
—— manifestation, 90, 283
—— response, 26
Enemies, 282
Energy, waste of, 219
Environment, 6
—— and food, 56
—— changes of, 283
—— external, conditions in, 279, 282
Equipment, hereditary, 6
Evolution of breeding stations or territory, 15, 19
—— of the territory, 176
—— of the voice, 163
Existence, struggle for, 294
Experience, acquired, 300
Experiments, removal of nests for, 181, 185, 190, 213, 214
Exposure, its effect on nestlings, 180
External environment, conditions in, 279, 282

Falcon, 48, 71
Feeding grounds, neutral, 125 in communities, 70 304 Females, fighting amongst, 109-118
—— sexual impulse of, 13
Fieldfare, 124
Fighting instinct, 79, 82
Flight, emotional behaviour of Godwit during, 53
Flocks, in winter, birds collect together in, 262
Flycatcher, 244
Food, procuring of, 5
—— abundance, or scarcity of, its relation to prosperity of young, 15, 16
—— its bearing, on the movement of flocks, 262
—— rearing of young dependent on rapid and regular, 179, 195
—— supply, proximity to, necessary for rearing young, 179, 195
Fortuitous mating, 174
Fowler, Ward, on the value of communities, Rooks, 202
Fulmar, 121, 247
Functional activity, 259

—— instinct of Reeve, 173
Functioning of the disposition, 275
—— of the primary dispositions, 100

Garden Warbler, 223, 225, 230
Gätke, H., *Birds of Heligoland*, 24
—— on the absence of song in birds on Heligoland, 124
—— on the early arrival of Guillemots on Heligoland, 64
Godwit, emotional behaviour of, during flight, 53
—— Black-tailed, 53
Grasshopper Warbler, 39, 131, 139, 153, 155, 187, 244
Greenfinch, 28, 33, 140, 235, 236
Gregarious instinct, 20, 61, 141, 265, 66, 269, 276, 289, 290, 291, 296, 300
Grouse, Black, 63
Guillemot, Bridled, 64
—— Common, 63, 64, 121, 192, 195, 206, 211, 247
—— Ringed, 64
Gull, Common, 119
—— Herring, 210, 278

Habit formation, law of, 8, 62, 65, 66, 67, 205
Hawfinch, 28
Headquarters, 176, 206, 207, 274
—— restricted, 8, 9, 30, 50, 58, 64, 127
Hedge-Sparrow, 213, 221, 244
Hereditary equipment, 6
Herring-Gull, 210, 278
Hooded-Crow, 202
Hostility and territory, relationship between, 242
House-Sparrow, 218

Imitation, vocal, powers of, 156, 157, 161
Impulse, internal, 279
—— to brood, 191
Inherited disposition, 5
Instinct, fighting, 79-82
—— gregarious, 20, 61, 141, 265, 266, 269, 276, 289, 290, 291, 296, 300
—— migratory, 37
—— of song related to establishment of territory, 125
—— sexual, reawakening of, 4, 18
Instinctive response, 180

Instincts susceptible to stimulation, 259
Internal impulse, 279 305 Internal stimulation, 62, 123
Interpretation of battles, 75
Intolerance of other birds, 218, 219
Intrusion resented, 274
Isolation, impulse to seek, 288
—— of male, 12, 62, 65, 73, 81
—— of male during breeding season, 267, 272, 273, 275, 281

Jay, 87, 156, 283

Kestrel, 228
Kittiwake, 116, 200, 247

Lapwing, 58, 59, 61, 62, 64, 84, 103, 104, 126, 189, 190, 220, 251, 284
Lapwing, life-history of, 58-61
Late arrival, advantages and disadvantages of, 33-44
Law of battle, 74, 75, 86
Lesser Whitethroat, 230, 244
Linnet, 156

M'Dougall, Dr, *Social Psychology*, 77
Magpie, 219, 283
Males arrive before advent of females, 24
Marsh-Warbler, 39, 40, 52, 81, 132, 140 153, 155, 156, 165, 225
Martin, 201, 218
Mating, difficulties of, 172
—— fortuitous, 174
Maximum number supportable in a given locality, 49
Meadow-Pipit, 188
Meeting places for antics, 54, 63
Mental Image, 77
Merlin, 227
Migration, 3-4
—— distance no criterion, 279
—— its relation to territory, 259
Migration, origin of, 260, 277
—— phenomenon of, 277
Migratory instinct, 37
—— species more highly specialised than resident species, 56
Missel-Thrush, 21
Mobility of the land and stability of the water, 260
Moor-hen, 61, 85, 103, 218, 250, 251
Morgan, Professor Lloyd, on instinctive behaviour, 74
—— on emotional behaviour, 114

Nest, cleaning of, 180
—— construction of, 3
Nests, removal of, for experiments, 181, 185, 190, 213, 214
Neutral feeding grounds, 62, 125
—— ground, 98
Newton, E., on the arrival at breeding stations of males before female, 24, 35
Nightingale, 39, 156
Notes of alarm, 119
—— of anger, 119
—— of recognition, 139
—— of warning, 119, 139, 141, 145, 151, 153

Offspring, rearing of, 3, 4
Organic change, sexual, 92, 123
—— changes, 65
—— condition of Reeve, 173
Owl, Wood, 156

Paired for life, 55-56
Parental instinctive response, failure of, 185
Partridge, 87, 218
Persecution, Carrion Crow and Magpie, 225 306 Persecution, Carrion Crow and Rook, 227
—— House Sparrow and Martin, 218
—— Lapwing and Snipe, 220
—— Raven and Buzzard, 217
—— —— and Peregrine, 216
—— Starling and Woodpecker, 218, 237
Persistency to remain in territory, 68
Pied-Wagtail, 86, 155
Pigeon, Wood, 219
Pipit, Meadow, 188
—— Tree, 51, 188, 189, 222, 244, 278
Polyandrous females, 144
Predatory species, 268
Promiscuous pairing of Ruffs, 172
Proximity to food-supply necessary for rearing young, 179, 195
Psychology, Manual of, 1
Puffin, 63, 116, 200
Pugnacious instinct, 87-109
Pugnacity, 11, 62
—— of females to obtain mates, 109-118
—— of males, prior to mating-season

77-81
—— of Moor-Hen, 218

Racial preparation, 41, 43, 46, 67, 205, 206, 266
Rail, Water, 218
Raven, 48, 202, 216
Razor-bill, 63, 64, 200, 247
Readjustment of territory, 146
Rearing of offspring, 3, 4
Red-backed Shrike, 39, 50, 51, 156
Redbreast, 47
Redshank, 139
Redwing, 124
Redstart, 230, 244
Reed-Bunting, 28, 68, 69, 85, 104, 132, 156, 158, 160, 244, 246, 273
Reed-Warbler, 49, 51, 68, 81, 132, 140, 152, 153, 211, 225
Reeve, 171
Relation of song to the territory, 119-68
—— of territory to migration, 259
—— of territory to the system of reproduction, 169-214
Relationship to a territory, 169
Reproduction, 14, 15
—— and territory, 169-214
—— attainment of, 2, 6, 37
—— goal of, 6
Ringed Guillemot, 64
Robbery of territory, 104-107
Rock-formation, suitability for Guillemots nesting on, 196
Rook, 202, 227
Routine behaviour, 262
Ruff, 54, 63, 172
—— meeting places for conflicts, 54
Ruffs, promiscuous pairing of, 172

Savi's Warbler, 139
Sedge-Warbler, 25, 44, 152, 226, 244
Selous, E., on the life-history of Ruffs and Reeves, 172
—— on meeting places for conflicts and antics, 54
—— on the meeting places of Black Grouse, 63
Service, Robert, on flocks of unmated Sedge-Warblers, 44, 45
Sexual behaviour, 3
—— conflicts, 10
—— development, 6
—— function, discharge of, 2, 3, 26
—— impulse of females, 13 307 Sex-

ual instinct in the migratory male, 26
—— of Reeve, 173
—— —— reawakening of, 4, 18
—— life of birds, 1
—— maturity, males arrive at, before females, 36
—— organic change, 92, 123
—— selection, 166
Shag, 121
Shrike, Red-backed, 39, 50, 51, 156
Skylark, 188, 236, 244
Snipe, 153, 156, 219, 220
Sociability when not paired, 125, 126
Song, as an aid in searching for a mate, 12
—— its influence on mating, 167
—— origin of, 138
—— relation to reproduction, 123
—— relation to territory, 119-168
—— volume of, influenced by age, seasonal sexual development, or isolation, 166
Song-Thrush, 222, 244
Sparrow, House, 218
Sparrow-Hawk, 269
Spring, at approach of, birds lose their shyness, 138
Stability of the water and mobility of the land, 260
Starling, 217, 218, 237, 251
Stimulation, internal, 62, 123
—— question of, 284
Stonechat, 87, 187, 188, 189, 222, 233, 234
Stout, Dr, *Manual of Psychology*, 1, 77
Struggle for existence, 294
Susceptibility to position, 96
Swallow, 21, 156, 278

Territory, 1, 5
—— adjustment of, 10
Territory and reproduction, 169-214
—— breeding, 2, 3, 7
—— dates of acquisition of, 33
—— defence of, 6
—— desertion of, after rearing young, 276
—— disposition to defend, 73-118
—— disposition to secure, 6, 20-72
—— establishment of, 74, 285
—— evolution of, 176
—— failure to secure, 286
—— fights for, 10, 11, 13, 62
—— ownership of, 189
—— possession of, a stimulus to song, 136
—— its relation to migration, 259
—— its relation to reproduction, 169-214
—— readjustment of, 147
—— restriction of, advantageous for mating, 172
—— restricted, 8, 9, 30, 50, 58, 64
—— separate for male and female Cuckoo, 144
—— song, its relation to the, 119-68
—— temporary desertion of, 28, 35, 58, 59
—— and hostility, relationship between, 242
Thrush, Song, 222, 244
Tit, Blue, 221, 226
—— Great, 221
—— Long-tailed, 226
Tradition, 300
Tree-Pipit, 51, 188, 189, 222, 232, 244, 278
Turtle-Dove, 126, 232

Union of sexes, 12
Ussher, H. B., on the hostility between Choughs and Hooded Crows and Choughs and Ravens, 227, 308

Vocal Imitation, 156, 157, 161
Voice calls of Curlew, 263

Wagtail, Pied, 86, 155
—— Yellow, 278
Wanderings from land, Guillemots, 193
Warbler, Garden, 223, 225, 230
—— Grasshopper, 39, 131, 139, 155, 187, 244
—— Marsh, 39, 40, 52, 81, 132, 140, 155, 156, 225
—— Reed, 49, 51, 68, 81, 132, 140, 152, 153, 211, 225
—— Savi's, 139
—— Sedge, 25, 44, 152, 226, 244
—— Willow, 25, 47, 50, 51, 80, 91, 140, 187, 211, 232, 244, 273
—— Wood, 50, 51, 132, 221
Warfare between different species and its relation to the territory, 215-58
Warning notes, 119
—— of danger, 269
Water Rail, 218
Wheatear, 25, 51
Whimbrel, 140

Whinchat, 39, 50, 51, 81, 222, 232, 233, 234, 244
Whitethroat, 25, 50, 68, 69, 124, 140, 182, 187, 189, 190, 213, 230, 244
—— Lesser, 230, 244
Wild Duck, 250
Will, the, to fight, 102
Willow-Warbler, 25, 47, 50, 51, 80, 91, 140, 187, 211, 232, 244, 273
Winter assemblies, 262-63
Witherby, H. F., in *British Birds*, on the return to former breeding-ground, 281
Wood-Owl, 156
Wood-Pigeon, 219
Wood-Warbler, 50, 51, 132, 221
Woodpecker, Lesser Spotted, 237
—— Great Spotted, 237, 238
—— Green, 20, 71, 156, 208, 218, 237
Wren, 244

Yellow Bunting, 28, 30, 47, 64, 140, 159, 162, 183, 187, 188, 189, 235, 236, 286
Young die in nest from exposure, 184, 185

PRINTED BY OLIVER AND BOYD, EDINBURGH, SCOTLAND